History 1
Student Guide

Part 2

About K12 Inc.

K12 Inc., a technology-based education company, is the nation's leading provider of proprietary curriculum and online education programs to students in grades K–12. K^{12} provides its curriculum and academic services to online schools, traditional classrooms, blended school programs, and directly to families. K12 Inc. also operates the K^{12} International Academy, an accredited, diploma-granting online private school serving students worldwide. K^{12}'s mission is to provide any child the curriculum and tools to maximize success in life, regardless of geographic, financial, or demographic circumstances. K12 Inc. is accredited by CITA. More information can be found at www.K12.com.

978-1-60153-311-1

Printed by R.R. Donnelley, Kendallville, IN, USA, May 2016

Table of Contents

Unit 8: Ancient China

Student Guide
Lesson 1. Optional: Ancient Crete

Travel back in time to ancient Greece. Meet the Greek gods and learn the legend of how the Trojan War began. Hear the tales of this war related by Homer in the *Illiad* and the *Odyssey*. Then let the games begin at the original Olympics!

Lesson Objectives

- Locate the Mediterranean Sea on the globe.
- Locate Crete on the map of Ancient Greece.
- Describe the people of Crete as shipbuilders and traders.
- Tell that some of the people of Crete were trained to be bull-jumpers.

PREPARE

Approximate lesson time is 60 minutes.

Materials

For the Student

- 🖳 map of Ancient Greece
- globe, inflatable - current
- map, world
- pencils, no. 2
- paper, 8 1/2" x 11"
- pencils, colored, 16 or more
- crayons, 16 or more
- paper, colored construction, 12"x12"
- 🖳 A Minoan Ship coloring sheet
- paper, colored construction, 12"x12" - black, cut into 4" square
- Elmer's Glue-All
- scissors, round-end safety

Keywords and Pronunciation

Crete (kreet)
Minoans (mih-NOH-uhns)
Minos (MIY-nuhs)

LEARN

Activity 1. Optional: Optional Lesson Instructions *(Online)*

This lesson is OPTIONAL. It is provided for students who seek enrichment or extra practice. You may skip this lesson.

If you choose to skip this lesson, then go to the Plan or Lesson Lists page and mark this lesson "Skipped" in order to proceed to the next lesson in the course.

Activity 2. Optional: Find Ancient Greece *(Online)*

Activity 3. Optional: The Minoans *(Online)*

Activity 4. Optional: The Shipbuilders *(Online)*

Activity 5. Optional: Bull-Jumping *(Online)*

Activity 6. Optional: Ancient Crete *(Online)*

Activity 7. Optional: History Record Book *(Offline)*

Activity 8. Optional: Daring Bull-Jumper *(Offline)*

Activity 9. Optional: A Minoan Ship *(Offline)*

Activity 10. Optional: Banner for Ancient Crete *(Offline)*

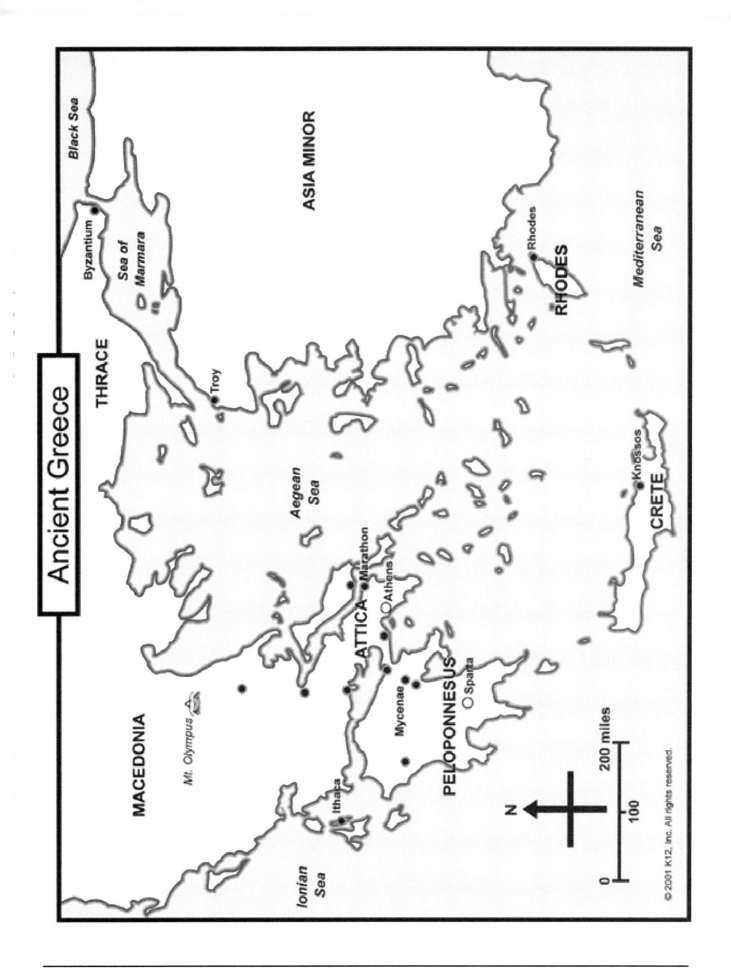

Ancient Greece

Black Sea

THRACE

Byzantium

Sea of Marmara

ASIA MINOR

Troy

MACEDONIA

Mt. Olympus

Aegean Sea

Marathon
Athens

ATTICA

Mycenae

Ithaca

PELOPONNESUS

Sparta

Ionian Sea

Mediterranean Sea

Rhodes

RHODES

Knossos

CRETE

N

0   100   200 miles

© 2001 K12, Inc. All rights reserved.

Student Guide
Lesson 2. Optional: Theseus and the Minotaur

King Minos built a huge palace at Knossos, decorated with paintings of Minoan life called frescoes. This palace may also have inspired the story of "Theseus and the Minotaur."

Lesson Objectives

- Locate the Aegean Sea on the map of Ancient Greece.
- Define labyrinth as a maze.
- Explain that the legend of the Minotaur is a made-up story about a monster that lived in Crete.

PREPARE

Approximate lesson time is 60 minutes.

Materials

For the Student

map of Ancient Greece

pencils, no. 2

paper, 8 1/2" x 11"

pencils, colored, 16 or more

Wings by Jane Yolen and Dennis Nolan

Keywords and Pronunciation

Aegeus (EE-joos)

Ariadne (ar-ee-AD-nee)

Knossos (NAH-suhs)

labyrinth (LA-buh-rinth)

Minotaur (MIH-nuh-tor)

Theseus (THEE-see-uhs)

LEARN
Activity 1. Optional: Optional Lesson Instructions *(Online)*

This lesson is OPTIONAL. It is provided for students who seek enrichment or extra practice. You may skip this lesson.

If you choose to skip this lesson, then go to the Plan or Lesson Lists page and mark this lesson "Skipped" in order to proceed to the next lesson in the course.

Activity 2. Optional: Find Crete *(Online)*

Activity 3. Optional: The Story of King Minos *(Online)*

Activity 4. Optional: Theseus and the Minotaur *(Online)*

Activity 5. Optional: History Record Book *(Offline)*

Activity 6. Optional: The Labyrinth *(Offline)*

Activity 7. Optional: Other Stories About King Minos *(Offline)*

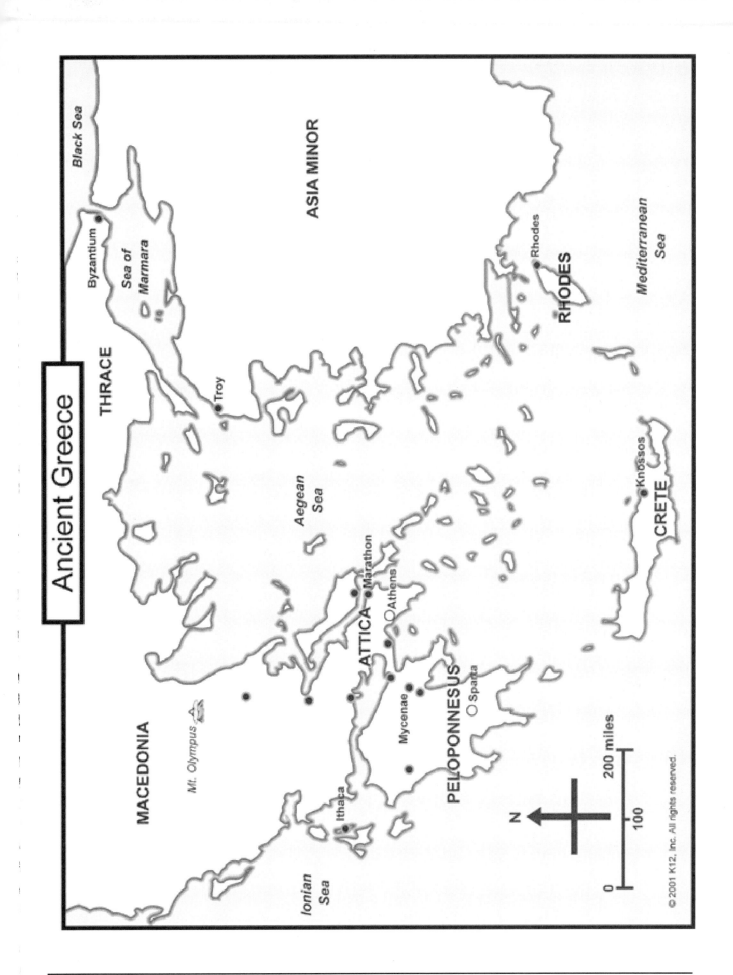

Ancient Greece

Black Sea

ASIA MINOR

THRACE

Byzantium

Sea of Marmara

Troy

Aegean Sea

MACEDONIA

Mt. Olympus

Ithaca

Ionian Sea

ATTICA

Marathon
Athens

PELOPONNESUS

Mycenae

Sparta

Rhodes

RHODES

Mediterranean Sea

Knossos

CRETE

N

0   100   200 miles

© 2001 K12, Inc. All rights reserved.

Student Guide
Lesson 3: Life in Ancient Greece

Jutting into the Mediterranean Sea is the large peninsula we now call Greece, a land that is rocky, mountainous, and hard to farm. In ancient times, Greece was a group of independent city-states, each with its own army, laws, and leaders. Shipbuilding and storytelling were very important in ancient Greece.

Lesson Objectives

- Locate Greece on a map.
- Explain that Greece was made up of many city-states.
- Describe the land in Greece as rocky and mountainous.
- Explain that much of the land in Greece was hard to farm.

PREPARE

Approximate lesson time is 60 minutes.

Advance Preparation

- If you choose to complete the optional mapmaking activity, have your student assist you as you prepare the salt dough.

  1. Mix 1 cup of flour and 1/2 cup salt together in a large bowl with a fork.
  2. In a cup, mix 1 tablespoon of water and 1/4 teaspoon of vegetable oil.
  3. Pour the wet ingredients over the dry ingredients in the bowl and stir with a fork until moistened. The dough will be somewhat dry. Don't worry! It will moisten as it sits in the refrigerator. (If it's too dry, add a couple of drops of water.)
  4. Split the mixture evenly into three cereal bowls.
  5. Add food coloring into the dough in each bowl to create colors for the map--blue for water and rivers, green for flat areas of land, and brown for mountainous areas.
  6. Place the dough from each cereal bowl into a separate sandwich bag.

Materials

For the Student

    🖳 map of Ancient Greece

globe, inflatable

map, world

pencils, no. 2

paper, 8 1/2" x 11"

pencils, colored, 16 or more

cardboard, boxes

flour - 1 cup

plastic sandwich bags, zipper-closed (3)

salt - 1/2 cup

bowl - cereal (3)

bowl - large

food coloring - green, blue, brown

fork

household items - oil, vegetable

plastic wrap

water - lukewarm, not hot

crayons, 16 or more

Growing Up in Ancient Greece by Chris Chelepi

LEARN
Activity 1: Find Greece *(Online)*

Activity 2: A Rough and Rocky Land *(Online)*

Activity 3: City-States *(Online)*

Activity 4: Shipbuilding and Storytelling *(Online)*

Activity 5: Life in Ancient Greece *(Online)*

Activity 6: History Record Book *(Offline)*

ASSESS

Lesson Assessment: Life in Ancient Greece (*Offline*)

You will complete an offline assessment covering the main objectives of this lesson. Your learning coach will score this assessment.

LEARN
Activity 7. Optional: Relief Map *(Offline)*

Activity 8. Optional: Greek: Mountains and Islands *(Offline)*

Activity 9. Optional: More About Life in Ancient Greece *(Offline)*

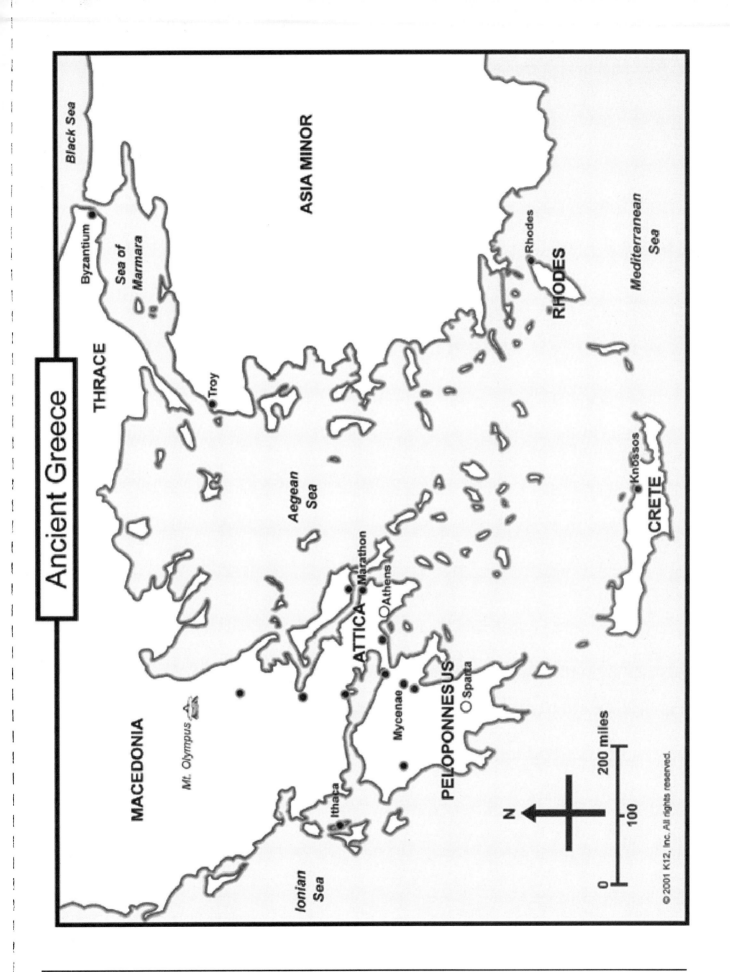

Ancient Greece

THRACE

MACEDONIA

ASIA MINOR

Black Sea

Byzantium

Sea of Marmara

Troy

Aegean Sea

Mt. Olympus

Ithaca

Ionian Sea

ATTICA

Marathon

Athens

Mycenae

PELOPONNESUS

Sparta

RHODES

Rhodes

Mediterranean Sea

Knossos

CRETE

N

0   100   200 miles

© 2001 K12, Inc. All rights reserved.

Lesson Assessment

Life in Ancient Greece

Use your world map to answer question 1.

1. Where is Greece located?

2. The cities in ancient Greece each governed themselves, with their own laws, armies, and leaders. What do we call these cities?

3. What is the land in Greece like?

4. Was the land in Greece easy to farm?

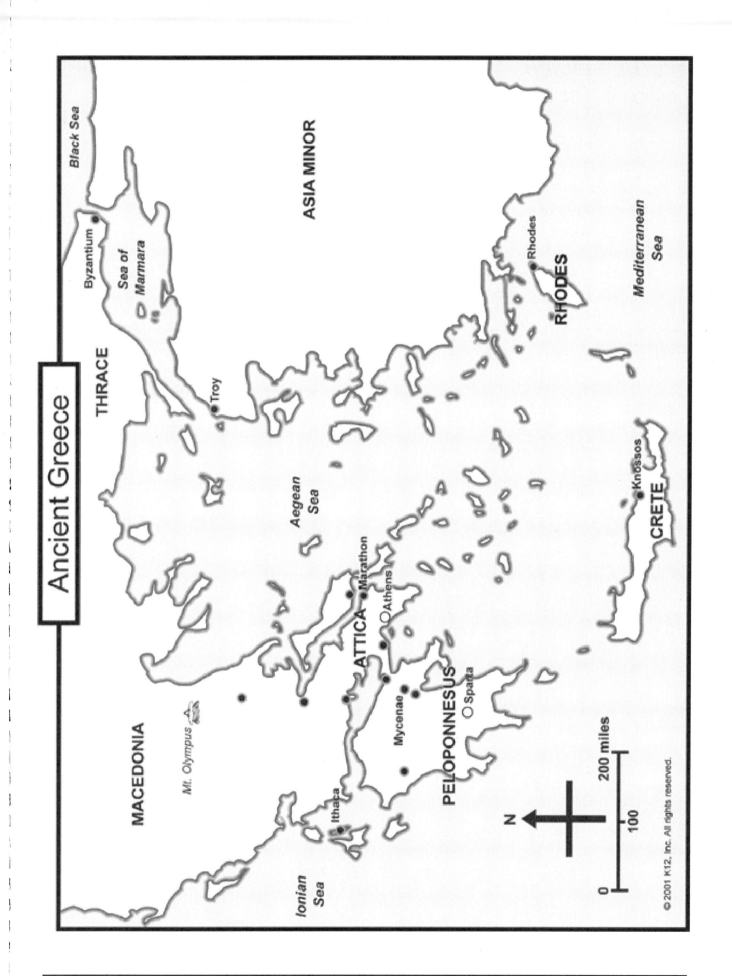

Ancient Greece

THRACE

Black Sea

Byzantium

Sea of Marmara

ASIA MINOR

Troy

Aegean Sea

Rhodes

RHODES

Mediterranean Sea

MACEDONIA

Mt. Olympus

Ithaca

ATTICA

Marathon

Athens

Mycenae

PELOPONNESUS

Sparta

Knossos

CRETE

Ionian Sea

N

0   100   200 miles

© 2001 K12, Inc. All rights reserved.

Student Guide
Lesson 4: The Greek Gods

The ancient Greeks believed in many gods and goddesses who made things happen on Earth. While these gods and goddesses often acted much like people, they were (the Greeks believed) immortal.

Lesson Objectives

- Explain that the ancient Greeks believed in many gods and goddesses.
- Identify Mount Olympus as the home of the Greek gods.
- Explain that while the Greek gods sometimes acted like people, the Greeks believed they were immortal and had amazing powers.
- Identify Zeus as king of the Greek gods.

PREPARE

Approximate lesson time is 60 minutes.

Materials

For the Student

  🖳 map of Ancient Greece

  pencils, no. 2

  paper, 8 1/2" x 11"

  pencils, colored, 16 or more

  🖳 Mount Olympus activity sheet

  crayons, 16 or more

  cardboard, sheets

  foil, aluminum

  markers, colored, 8 or more

  scissors, round-end safety

  tape, clear

  The Gods and Goddesses of Olympus by Aliki

Keywords and Pronunciation

ambrosia (am-BROH-zhuh)

Aphrodite (a-fruh-DIY-tee)

Athena (uh-THEE-nuh)

Hades (HAY-deez)

Hera (HAIR-uh)

Poseidon (puh-SIY-dn)

Zeus (zoos)

LEARN
Activity 1: Find Greece *(Online)*

Activity 2: Mount Olympus, Home of the Gods *(Online)*

Activity 3: The Gods and Goddesses *(Online)*

Activity 4: The Greek Gods *(Online)*

Activity 5: History Record Book *(Offline)*

Activity 6. Optional: Mount Olympus *(Offline)*

ASSESS

Lesson Assessment: The Greek Gods (*Online*)
You will complete an offline assessment covering the main objectives of this lesson. Your learning coach will score this assessment.

LEARN
Activity 7. Optional: Lightning Bolt, Trident, Spear *(Offline)*

Activity 8. Optional: Greek Stories *(Offline)*

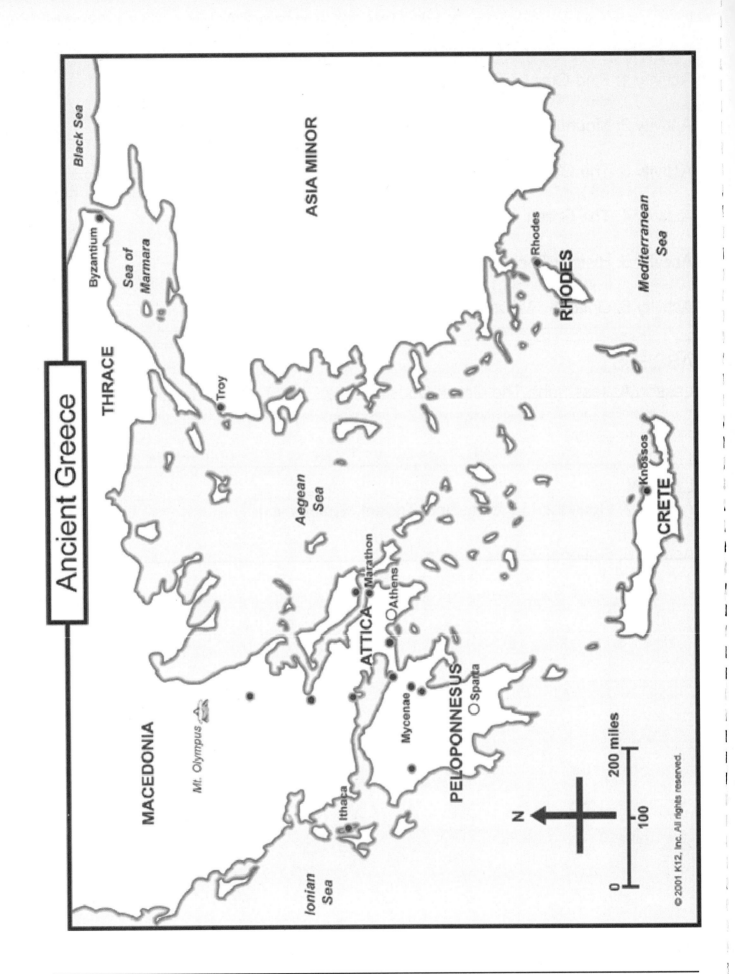

Ancient Greece

Black Sea

ASIA MINOR

THRACE

Byzantium

Sea of Marmara

Mediterranean Sea

Rhodes

RHODES

MACEDONIA

Troy

Mt. Olympus

Aegean Sea

Knossos

CRETE

Marathon

Athens

ATTICA

Mycenae

PELOPONNESUS

Sparta

Ithaca

Ionian Sea

N

0   100   200 miles

© 2001 K12, Inc. All rights reserved.

Lesson Assessment

The Greek Gods

1. Did the ancient Greeks believe in one or many gods?

2. Where did the gods and goddesses live?

3. How were the Greek gods and goddesses like people? How were the Greek gods and goddesses different from people?

4. Who was king of the gods?

Student Guide
Lesson 5: The Judgment of Paris

The ancient Greeks believed that their gods and goddesses often caused things to happen on Earth. They told the story of the Judgment of Paris to explain the beginnings of an important struggle, the Trojan War.

Lesson Objectives

- Identify the main points of the myth the Greeks told to explain the beginnings of the Trojan War, such as the argument over who should receive the golden apple and how Paris took Helen to Troy.
- Name the Greeks and the Trojans as the people who fought each other in the Trojan War.

PREPARE

Approximate lesson time is 60 minutes.

Materials

For the Student

    🖳 map of Ancient Greece

    pencils, no. 2

    paper, 8 1/2" x 11"

    pencils, colored, 16 or more

    paintbrush

    paper, colored construction, 12"x12"

    glitter

    markers, colored, 8 or more

    paints, watercolor, 8 colors or more

    popsicle sticks

    scissors, round-end safety

    tape, clear

    🖳 Trojan War activity sheet

    paper, colored construction, 12"x12" - white (3)

    stapler

    She and He: Adventures in Mythology by Jim Weiss

Keywords and Pronunciation

Eris (EE-ris)

Menelaus (me-nl-AY-uhs)

Peleus (PEE-lee-uhs)

Thetis (THEE-tuhs)

LEARN
Activity 1: Greek Gods and Goddesses *(Online)*

Activity 2: The Judgment of Paris *(Online)*

Activity 3: The Judgment of Paris *(Online)*

Activity 4: History Record Book *(Offline)*

Activity 5. Optional: Make a Mural *(Offline)*

Activity 6. Optional: Trojan War Mini-Book *(Offline)*

ASSESS
Lesson Assessment: The Judgment of Paris (*Offline*)
You will complete an offline assessment covering the main objectives of this lesson. Your learning coach will score this assessment.

LEARN
Activity 7. Optional: Hear More Myths *(Offline)*

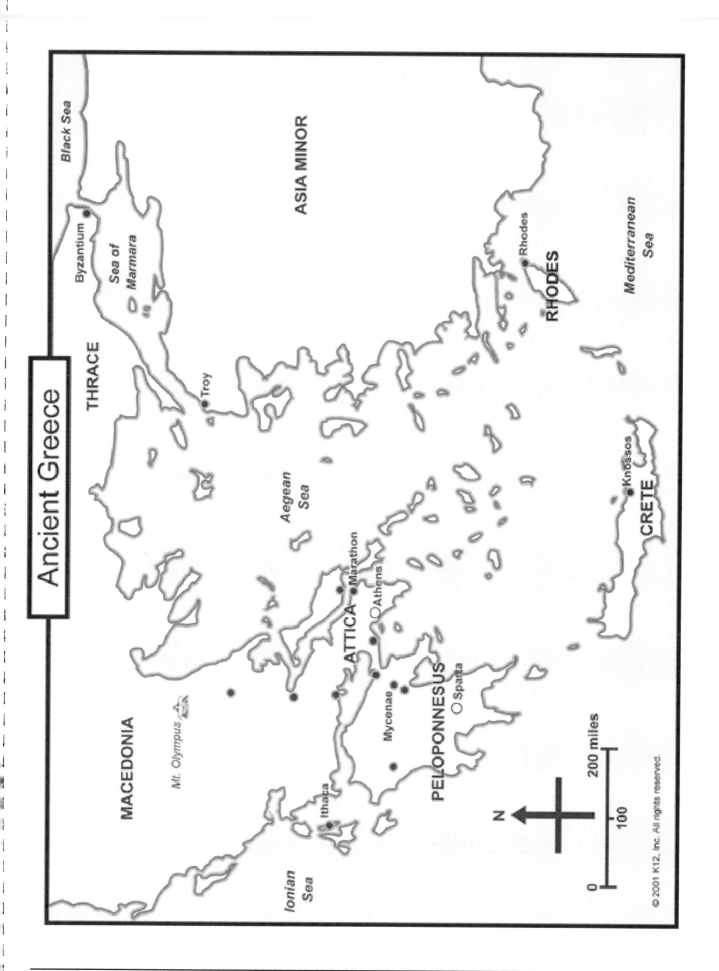

Ancient Greece

MACEDONIA

THRACE

Black Sea

Byzantium

Sea of Marmara

ASIA MINOR

Troy

Mt. Olympus

Aegean Sea

Rhodes

RHODES

Mediterranean Sea

Ithaca

Ionian Sea

Mycenae

PELOPONNESUS

Sparta

ATTICA

Marathon

Athens

Knossos

CRETE

N

0   100   200 miles

© 2001 K12, Inc. All rights reserved.

Trojan War Activity Sheet

Use the sentences below to create your mini-book about the Trojan War.

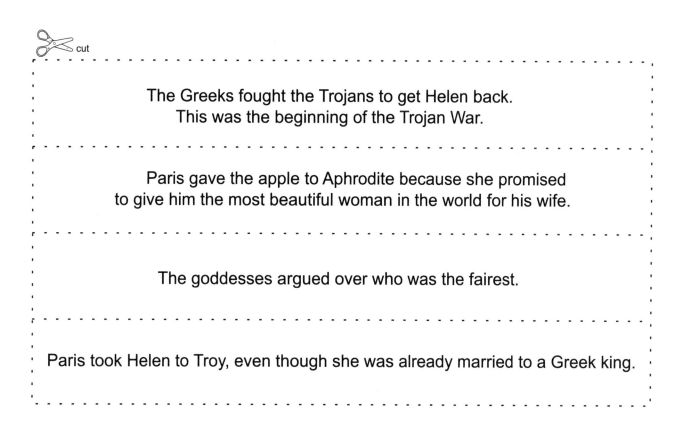

✂ cut

The Greeks fought the Trojans to get Helen back.
This was the beginning of the Trojan War.

Paris gave the apple to Aphrodite because she promised
to give him the most beautiful woman in the world for his wife.

The goddesses argued over who was the fairest.

Paris took Helen to Troy, even though she was already married to a Greek king.

Lesson Assessment

The Judgment of Paris

1. Who chose which goddess should receive the golden apple?

2. According to the myth, why did the Trojan War start?

3. Why did Paris choose Aphrodite?

4. Who was the most beautiful woman in the world?

5. Where did Paris take the most beautiful woman?

6. Who fought against each other in the Trojan War?

Student Guide
Lesson 6: The Trojan War: Part 1

The Greeks fought a long war against the Trojans, called the Trojan War. Today we begin reading a book that tells the story of that war.

Lesson Objectives

- Find Troy on the map of Ancient Greece.
- Identify Priam as the king of the Trojans.

PREPARE

Approximate lesson time is 60 minutes.

Advance Preparation

- If you don't have it already, please gather the book *The Trojan Horse* by Emily Little (ISBN 0394896742).

Materials

For the Student

- map of Ancient Greece
- globe, inflatable
- The Trojan Horse Discussion Questions
- The Trojan Horse by Emily Little (ISBN 0394896742)
- pencils, no. 2
- paper, 8 1/2" x 11"
- pencils, colored, 16 or more
- map of the Trojan War
- crayons, 16 or more
- markers, colored, 8 or more
- Fighting the Trojan War activity sheet

Keywords and Pronunciation

Agamemnon (a-guh-MEM-nahn)

Ithaca (IH-thi-kuh)

Menelaus (me-nl-AY-uhs)

Mycenae (miy-SEE-nee)

Odysseus (oh-DIH-see-uhs)

Priam (PRIY-uhm)

LEARN
Activity 1: A Golden Apple Leads to War *(Online)*

Activity 2: Sailing the Seas *(Online)*

Activity 3: The Trojan Horse *(Offline)*

Activity 4: The Trojan War: Part 1 *(Online)*

Activity 5: History Record Book *(Offline)*

Activity 6. Optional: Sea Routes to Troy *(Offline)*

ASSESS
Lesson Assessment: The Trojan War, Part 1 (*Offline*)
You will complete an offline assessment covering the main objectives of this lesson. Your learning coach will score this assessment.

LEARN
Activity 7. Optional: Fighting the Trojan War *(Offline)*

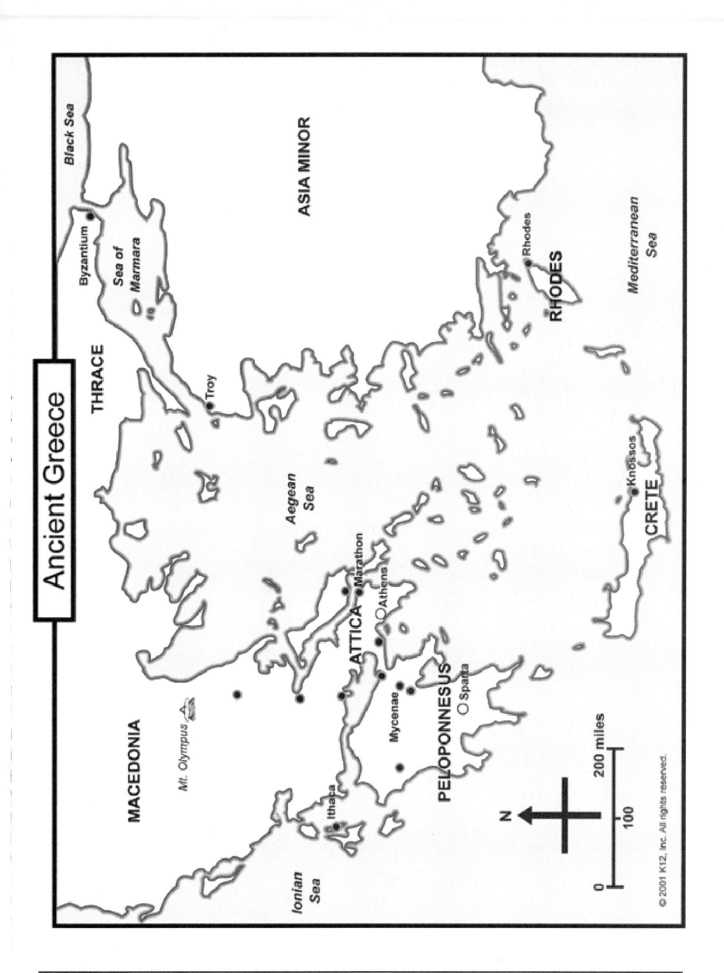

Ancient Greece

Black Sea

ASIA MINOR

THRACE

Byzantium

Sea of
Marmara

MACEDONIA

Troy

Mt. Olympus

Aegean
Sea

Rhodes

RHODES

Mediterranean
Sea

Knossos

CRETE

ATTICA

Marathon

Athens

Mycenae

PELOPONNESUS

Sparta

Ithaca

Ionian
Sea

N

200 miles

100

0

© 2001 K12, Inc. All rights reserved.

The Trojan Horse Discussion Questions

Read aloud Chapters 1 and 2 of *The Trojan Horse*. Ask the discussion questions as you read.

After reading pages 6 and 7, ask the question:
Why did the Trojans build a wall around their city?

to protect the city against enemies

After reading page 8, ask the question:
What is the only way to get in and out of the city?

through a big gate in the walls

Page 9 refers to a "hostile" army. After reading this section, ask the question:
What do you think "hostile" means?

unfriendly

After reading page 12, ask the questions:
Why are the Greeks angry with the Trojans?
Who is the king of the Trojans?

The Trojans force them to pay a toll to sail past Troy. Priam (PRIY-uhm) is the king of the Trojans.

Page 13 refers to Menelaus planning his "revenge." After reading this section, ask the question:
What is "revenge"?

getting even, or getting back at someone for something bad done to you

After reading page 14, ask the question:
What has happened to Helen in this story?

She has been kidnapped by the Trojans.

After reading page 22, ask the question:
Who wins when the Greeks and Trojans first battle?

No one wins.

After completing Chapter 2, ask the child to predict what the Greeks will do next to get into the city.

Sea Routes to Troy

Show where Ithaca, Mycenae, Sparta, and Troy were located by filling in each circle on the map with a different color. Complete the legend using these same colors. Draw the routes you think the Greek warships might have taken from each of the three city-states to Troy.

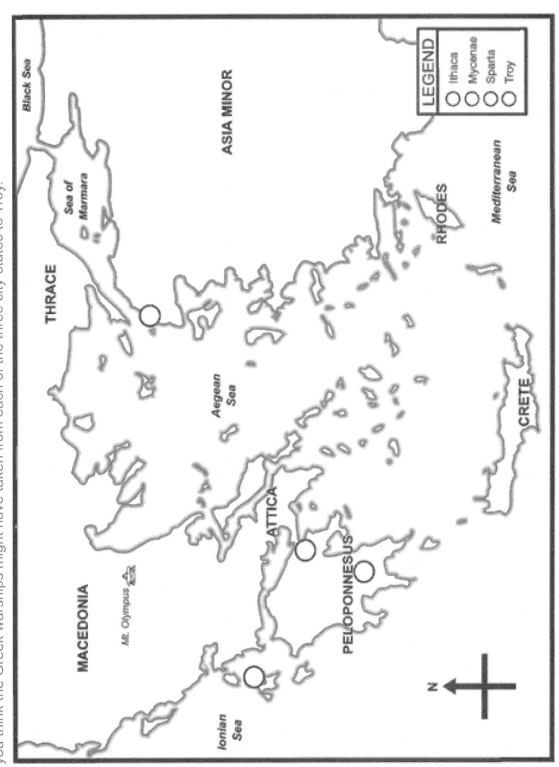

Name _____ Date _____

Lesson Assessment

The Trojan War, Part 1

Use your map of Ancient Greece to answer question 1.

1. Where is Troy located?

2. Who was the king of the Trojans?

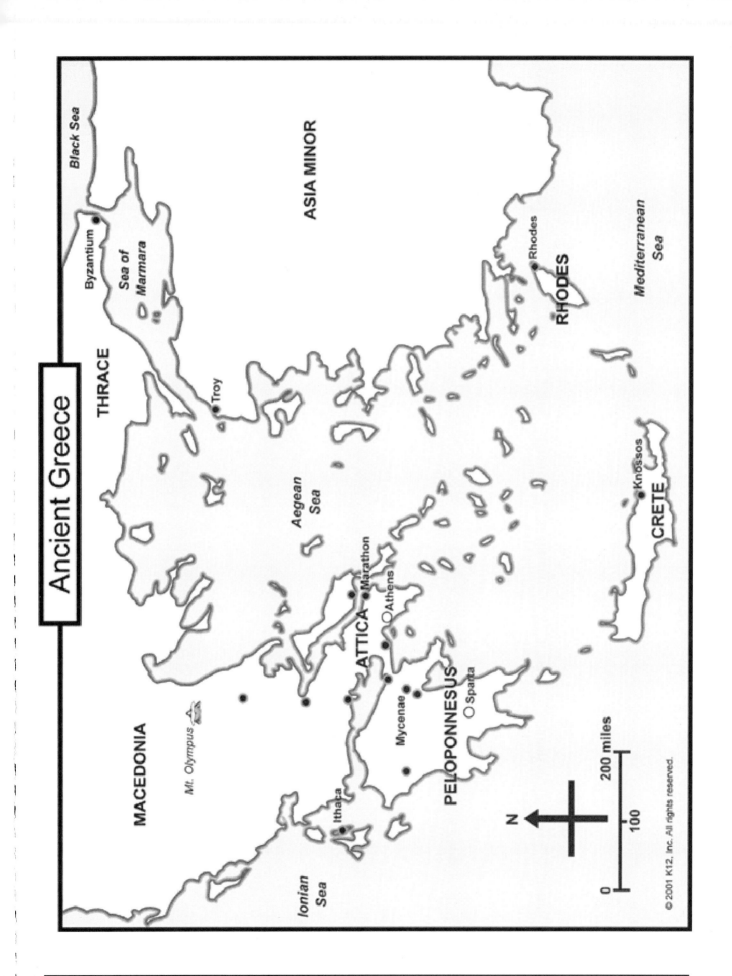

Ancient Greece

Black Sea

THRACE

MACEDONIA

Byzantium

Sea of Marmara

Troy

ASIA MINOR

Mt. Olympus

Aegean Sea

Rhodes

RHODES

Mediterranean Sea

Ionian Sea

Ithaca

ATTICA

Marathon

Athens

Mycenae

PELOPONNESUS

Sparta

Knossos

CRETE

N

0   100   200 miles

© 2001 K12, inc. All rights reserved.

Fighting the Trojan War

Look at each picture on the activity sheet and think back to the story. When you look at each picture, do you think of Greece or Troy? If you think of Greece, label the picture with a "G." If you think of Troy, write a "T." Then color the pictures.

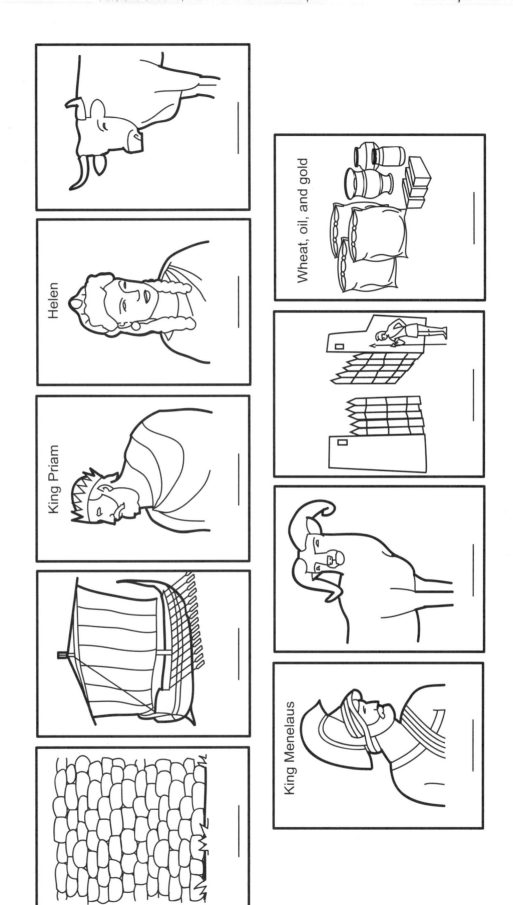

Student Guide
Lesson 7: The Trojan War: Part 2

The Greeks fought a long war against the Trojans, called the Trojan War. The story of the Trojan War is recounted by the great Greek poet Homer in an epic poem called the *Iliad*.

Lesson Objectives

- Identify Odysseus as a Greek hero.
- Identify Homer as a Greek poet and author of the *Iliad*.
- Retell the story of the Trojan Horse.

PREPARE

Approximate lesson time is 60 minutes.

Materials

For the Student

The Trojan Horse by Emily Little (ISBN 0394896742)

🖳 More Trojan Horse Discussion Questions

pencils, no. 2

paper, 8 1/2" x 11"

pencils, colored, 16 or more

crayons, 16 or more

index cards, 4" x 6"

🖳 Trojan Horse Cut-Out

paper, heavy

stapler

markers, colored, 8 or more

Black Ships Before Troy: The Story of the Iliad by Rosemary Sutcliffe

Keywords and Pronunciation

Cassandra (kuh-SAN-druh)

Iliad (IL-ee-uhd)

Odysseus (oh-DIH-see-uhs)

Sinon (SIY-nahn)

LEARN
Activity 1: The City of Troy *(Offline)*

Activity 2: How the Greeks Won the War *(Offline)*

Activity 3: The Trojan War: Part 2 *(Online)*

Activity 4: History Record Book *(Offline)*

Activity 5. Optional: Story Shuffle *(Offline)*

Activity 6. Optional: The Trojan Horse *(Offline)*

ASSESS

Lesson Assessment: The Trojan War, Part 2 (*Offline*)

You will complete an offline assessment covering the main objectives of this lesson. Your learning coach will score this assessment.

LEARN

Activity 7. Optional: Discovering Troy *(Offline)*

Activity 8. Optional: More Stories of the Trojan War *(Offline)*

More Trojan Horse Discussion Questions

Read aloud Chapters 3 through 6 of *The Trojan Horse.* Ask the discussion questions as you read.

After reading page 29, ask the questions:
Who thought of the plan to build the wooden horse?
Who is hiding inside the horse?
Where are the rest of the Greeks?

Odysseus. Odysseus and his soldiers. They sailed past a nearby island and stopped.

After reading page 31, ask the question:
What do you think the Trojans will do?

After reading page 32, ask the question:
Why does King Priam decide not to destroy the horse?

Sinon told King Priam that the horse is a gift for Athena, and he does not want to make Athena angry.

After reading page 33, ask the questions:
Do you think the Trojans should take the wooden horse into their city?
What do you think will happen next?

After reading page 37, ask the questions:
What does Cassandra (kuh-SAN-druh) try to tell the Trojans? Do they listen?

Cassandra tries to tell the Trojans that "doom is near," but they pay no attention.

After reading page 43, ask the question:
How do the Greeks defeat the Trojans?

The Greeks climb out of the horse and set fires.

After reading page 46, ask the questions:
What did Homer do? What is the name of his long poem about the Trojan War?

Homer told about the Trojan War in his long poem called the Iliad.

Trojan Horse Cutout

✂ cut

Lesson Assessment

The Trojan War, Part 2

1. How did the Greeks plan to get inside Troy?

2. After the Trojans pulled the horse inside the city, what happened?

3. Who thought up the plan to build the wooden horse?

4. What is the title of Homer's long poem about the Trojan War?

5. Who won the Trojan War—the Trojans or Greeks?

Student Guide
Lesson 8: Homer's Great Greek Epics

Lesson Objectives

- Name Homer as the poet who wrote the *Iliad* and the *Odyssey*.
- Explain that the *Iliad* is about the Trojan War.
- Explain that the *Odyssey* is about Odysseus's journey home.

PREPARE

Approximate lesson time is 60 minutes.

Materials

For the Student

- 🖥 map of Ancient Greece
  crayons, 16 or more
  pencils, no. 2
  paper, 8 1/2" x 11"
  paper, colored construction, 12"x12"
  Classic Myths to Read Aloud by William F. Russell
  The Children's Homer: The Adventures of Odysseus and the Tale of Troy by Padraic Colum
  The Iliad and the Odyssey retold by Marcia Williams

Keywords and Pronunciation

Aeolus (EE-uh-luhs)
Iliad (IL-ee-uhd)
Illium (IL-ee-um)
Odysseus (oh-DIH-see-uhs)
Odyssey (AH-duh-see)

LEARN
Activity 1: A Greek Review *(Online)*

Activity 2: Homer the Poet *(Online)*

Activity 3: Homer's Great Greek Epics *(Online)*

Activity 4: History Record Book *(Offline)*

Activity 5. Optional: Storytelling *(Offline)*

ASSESS

Lesson Assessment: Homer's Great Greek Epics (*Offline*)

You will complete an offline assessment covering the main objectives of this lesson. Your learning coach will score this assessment.

LEARN

Activity 6. Optional: Come Hear Homer Poster *(Offline)*

Activity 7. Optional: Retellings of the *Odyssey* *(Offline)*

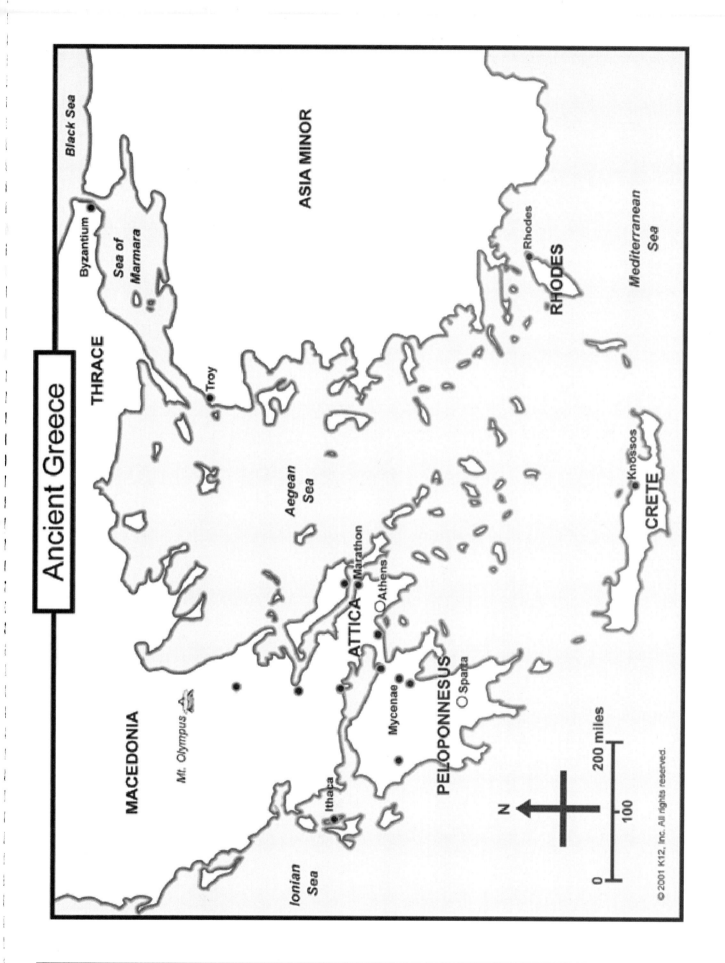

Ancient Greece

THRACE

Black Sea

Byzantium

Sea of Marmara

ASIA MINOR

Troy

Rhodes

RHODES

Mediterranean Sea

MACEDONIA

Mt. Olympus

Aegean Sea

Knossos

CRETE

ATTICA

Marathon

Athens

Mycenae

Sparta

PELOPONNESUS

Ithaca

Ionian Sea

N

0   100   200 miles

© 2001 K12, Inc. All rights reserved.

55

Lesson Assessment

Homer's Great Greek Epics

1. Who is the great Greek poet who wrote the *Iliad* and the *Odyssey*?

2. What is the *Iliad* about?

3. What is the *Odyssey* about?

Student Guide
Lesson 9: Let the Olympic Games Begin!

The Olympic Games began in ancient Greece as a celebration in honor of Zeus. Greek men participated in many games, testing their strength, speed, and courage for a chance to win the olive wreath of victory.

Lesson Objectives
- Explain that the first Olympic games were held in ancient Greece.
- Describe the original Olympics as athletic games.

PREPARE

Approximate lesson time is 60 minutes.

Materials
  For the Student
    map, world
    crayons, 16 or more
    pencils, no. 2
    paper, 8 1/2" x 11"
    paper, colored construction, 12"x12"
    newspaper - or magazines

Keywords and Pronunciation
Olympics : An ancient Panhellenic festival held every fourth year and made up of contests of sports, music, and literature with the victor's prize a crown of wild olive.

pentathlon (pen-TATH-luhn)

LEARN
Activity 1: A Greek Review *(Online)*

Activity 2: The Olympics *(Online)*

Activity 3: Let the Olympic Games Begin! *(Online)*

Activity 4: History Record Book *(Offline)*

Activity 5. Optional: Carry the Torch *(Offline)*

Activity 6. Optional: A Pentathlon *(Offline)*

ASSESS

Lesson Assessment: Let the Olympic Games Begin! (*Offline*)

You will complete an offline assessment covering the main objectives of this lesson. Your learning coach will score this assessment.

LEARN

Activity 7. Optional: Home Olympics *(Offline)*

Name _____   Date _____

Lesson Assessment

Let the Olympic Games Begin!

1. Where were the first Olympic games held?

2. What were the original Olympics?

Student Guide
Lesson 10: Greek Myths: Arachne and King Midas

The ancient Greeks told stories, called myths, about their gods and goddesses. Some myths explained how things came to be, while others showed what happened when people made unwise decisions.

Lesson Objectives

- Explain that the Greek myth of Arachne tells how spiders came to be.
- Tell that the stories about the Greek gods and goddesses are called myths.
- Tell that the phrase golden touch comes from the Greek myth about King Midas.

PREPARE

Approximate lesson time is 60 minutes.

Materials

For the Student

Greek Myths CD by Jim Weiss

pencils, no. 2

paper, 8 1/2" x 11"

pencils, colored, 16 or more

📖 Arachne as a Spider activity sheet

paper, colored construction, 12"x12" - yellow

markers, colored, 8 or more

King Midas and the Golden Touch by Charlotte Craft

Keywords and Pronunciation

Arachne (uh-RAK-nee)

Dionysus (diy-uh-NIY-suhs)

Midas (MIY-duhs)

LEARN
Activity 1: Greek Gods and Goddesses *(Online)*

Activity 2: Greek Myths *(Online)*

Activity 3: The Myth of Arachne *(Offline)*

Activity 4: King Midas *(Offline)*

Activity 5: Greek Myths: Arachne and King Midas *(Online)*

Activity 6: History Record Book *(Offline)*

Activity 7. Optional: Arachne as a Spider *(Offline)*

Activity 8. Optional: Midas Madness *(Offline)*

ASSESS

Lesson Assessment: Greek Myths: Arachne and King Midas *(Offline)*

You will complete an offline assessment covering the main objectives of this lesson. Your learning coach will score this assessment.

LEARN
Activity 9. Optional: Read On! *(Offline)*

Name _____ Date _____

Arachne as a Spider

Look at the picture of Arachne, the spider. In the thought bubble above her head, draw or write what she might be thinking about her change from person to spider.

Name _____ Date _____

Lesson Assessment

Greek Myths: Arachne and King Midas

1. What are the stories about the Greek gods and goddesses called?

2. What power did King Midas ask the god Dionysus to give him?

3. The story of Arachne explains how what creature came to be?

Student Guide
Lesson 11: Greek Myths: Heroes and Monsters

Some of the ancient Greek myths are about battles, monsters, and heroes. In ancient Greece, a hero had to be brave, strong, and able to do amazing deeds.

Lesson Objectives

- Demonstrate mastery of important knowledge and skills taught in this unit.
- Identify Perseus as the hero in a Greek myth who slays the monster Medusa.
- Define heroes in Greek myths as strong, brave characters who do amazing deeds.
- Explain that some Greek myths are about heroes and monsters.
- Locate the Mediterranean Sea on the globe.
- Explain that Greece was made up of many city-states.
- Explain that the ancient Greeks believed in many gods and goddesses.
- Identify Mount Olympus as the home of the Greek gods.
- Identify Zeus as king of the Greek gods.
- Name the Greeks and the Trojans as the people who fought each other in the Trojan War.
- Retell the story of the Trojan Horse.
- Name Homer as the poet who wrote the *Iliad* and the *Odyssey*.
- Explain that the *Iliad* is about the Trojan War.
- Explain that the first Olympic games were held in ancient Greece.
- Tell that the stories about the Greek gods and goddesses are called myths.
- Tell that the phrase golden touch comes from the Greek myth about King Midas.

PREPARE

Approximate lesson time is 60 minutes.

Materials

For the Student

Greek Myths CD by Jim Weiss

pencils, no. 2

paper, 8 1/2" x 11"

pencils, colored, 16 or more

crayons, 16 or more

paper, colored construction, 12"x12"

plates, paper

tissue paper

Elmer's Glue-All

scissors, round-end safety

   Greek Heroes coloring sheet

Keywords and Pronunciation
Hercules (HUR-kyuh-leez)
Hermes (HUR-meez)
Medusa (mih-DOO-suh)
Perseus (PUR-see-uhs)

LEARN
Activity 1: Greek Myths *(Online)*

Activity 2: Greek Heroes and Monsters *(Online)*

Activity 3: The Myth of Perseus and Medusa *(Online)*

Activity 4: Greek Myths: Heroes and Monsters *(Online)*

Activity 5: History Record Book *(Offline)*

Activity 6. Optional: A Medusa Mask *(Offline)*

Activity 7: Reviewing Unit Five *(Online)*

ASSESS
Unit Assessment: Ancient Greece, Part I: The Land and the Myths *(Offline)*
Complete an offline Unit Assessment. Your learning coach will score this part of the Assessment.

LEARN
Activity 8. Optional: Adventures of Hercules *(Offline)*

Activity 9. Optional: Ancient Heroes *(Offline)*

Name _____   Date _____

Ancient Greece, Part I: The Land and Myths

Select the one best answer. Shade or color the bubble for the answer you choose.

1. This body of water was very important to the ancient Greeks. They sailed on its waters to travel and to trade with other lands.
   - ○ Nile River
   - ○ Mediterranean Sea
   - ○ Euphrates River

2. What was Greece made up of?
   - ○ many good farms
   - ○ a single country
   - ○ many city-states

3. What was the home of the Greek gods?
   - ○ Mount Olympus
   - ○ Tower of Babel
   - ○ Crete

4. Who fought each other in the Trojan War?
   - ○ Greeks and Babylonians
   - ○ Trojans and Babylonians
   - ○ Greeks and Trojans

5. What do we call stories that explain how things came to be?
   - ○ myths
   - ○ poems
   - ○ fables

6. Which of these phrases comes from the Greek myth about King Midas?

- ○ feather touch
- ○ golden touch
- ○ golden eggs

7. What did the ancient Greeks believe in?

- ○ one god
- ○ many gods
- ○ three gods

8. What games did the ancient Greeks give the world?

- ○ football
- ○ soccer
- ○ Olympics

9. What were some Greek myths about?

- ○ heroes and monsters
- ○ roads and temples
- ○ land and water

10. Who was the king of the Greek gods?

- ○ Zeus
- ○ Poseidon
- ○ Homer

11. What does the poem called the *Iliad* tell the story of?

- ○ the Trojan War
- ○ why we have seasons
- ○ the adventures of Perseus

12. Who was the Greek poet of the *Odyssey*?
    ○ Homer
    ○ Minos
    ○ Midas

13. What was the Trojan Horse?
    ○ a flying horse that lived on Mount Olympus
    ○ a giant magical horse tamed by the sea god, Poseidon
    ○ a way for Greek soldiers to sneak inside and attack the city of Troy

14. Who was Perseus?
    ○ a hero in a Greek myth
    ○ the author of a Greek myth
    ○ a monster in a Greek myth

Greek Heroes

Two of these pictures are of Perseus, and two are of Hercules. Decide which they are, and write the hero's name under each picture. Then color the pictures of Perseus and Hercules on the coloring sheet.

Student Guide
Lesson 1: Athena Gets a City

Learn about Greek city-states and the differences between two strong rivals, Athens and Sparta. Then travel to the Persian Empire and meet Darius, the ruler who waged war against Greece. Meet the philosophers Socrates, Plato, and Aristotle. Learn how the Greeks fought each other during the Peloponnesian War but were later conquered by Alexander the Great.

The city of Athens was named after Athena, the goddess of wisdom. The ancient Athenians told a story about why their city was named after Athena.

Lesson Objectives

- Explain that Athens is named after the goddess Athena.
- Explain that Athena's gift to the people of Athens was the olive tree.
- Identify Athena as the ancient Greek goddess of wisdom.
- Identify Poseidon as the ancient Greek god of the sea.

PREPARE

Approximate lesson time is 60 minutes.

Materials

For the Student

    🖥 map of Ancient Greece

    crayons, 16 or more

    pencils, no. 2

    paper, 8 1/2" x 11"

    🖥 Poseidon and Athena activity sheet

    pencils, colored, 16 or more

    paper, colored construction, 12"x12" - white

LEARN
Activity 1: A Review of Greek Gods and Goddesses *(Online)*

Activity 2: Athena Gets a City *(Online)*

Activity 3: Athena Gets a City *(Online)*

Activity 4: History Record Book *(Offline)*

Activity 5. Optional: Gifts From Poseidon and Athena *(Offline)*

Activity 6. Optional: Poseidon or Athena *(Online)*

ASSESS

Lesson Assessment: Athena Gets a City (*Offline*)

You will complete an offline assessment covering the main objectives of this lesson. Your learning coach will score this assessment.

LEARN

Activity 7. Optional: Welcome to My Town *(Offline)*

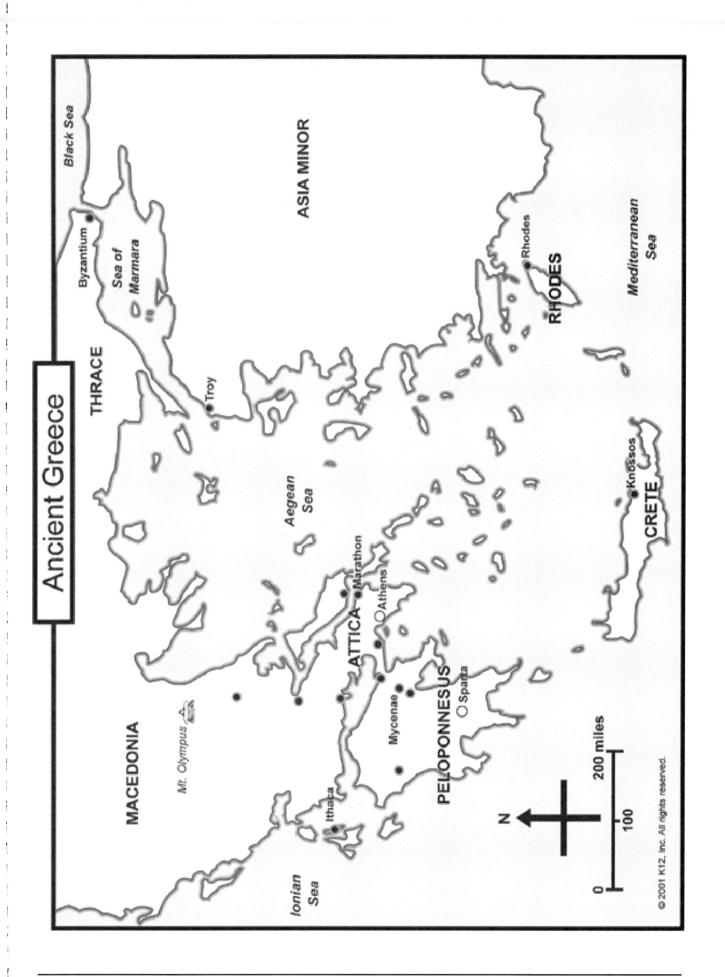

Ancient Greece

THRACE

Black Sea

Byzantium

Sea of Marmara

ASIA MINOR

MACEDONIA

Troy

Mt. Olympus

Ithaca

Ionian Sea

Aegean Sea

ATTICA

Marathon

Athens

Mycenae

PELOPONNESUS

Sparta

RHODES

Rhodes

Mediterranean Sea

CRETE

Knossos

N

0   100   200 miles

© 2001 K12, Inc. All rights reserved.

Name: _____

Goddess of: _____

Name: _____

God of: _____

Name _____ Date _____

Lesson Assessment

Athena Gets a City

1. Who is the city of Athens named after?

2. What gift did Athena bring to the mortals?

3. What was Athena the goddess of?

4. What was Poseidon the god of?

Student Guide
Lesson 2: Athens and Democracy

Athens introduced the world to a new form of government, *democracy*, or rule by the people. Each citizen cast his vote to help make decisions about law and government.

Lesson Objectives

- Locate Athens on a map.
- Define democracy as the people rule.
- Describe ancient Athens as a democracy.

PREPARE

Approximate lesson time is 60 minutes.

Materials

For the Student

- map of Ancient Greece
- crayons, 16 or more
- History Record Book
- pencils, no. 2
- paper, 8 1/2" x 11"
- pencils, colored, 16 or more
- Athens Travel Brochure coloring sheet
- Athens: Democracy on the Aegean cut-out sheet
- glue sticks
- index cards, 4" x 6"
- scissors, round-end safety

Keywords and Pronunciation

agora (A-guh-ruh)
democracy : rule by the people
Diocles (DIY-uh-kleez)
Nicomachus (nuh-KAHM-uh-kuhs)
obol (AH-buhl)

LEARN
Activity 1: Athens and Athena *(Online)*

Activity 2: Athens: From King to Democracy *(Online)*

Activity 3: A Vote in the Assembly *(Online)*

Activity 4: Athens and Democracy *(Online)*

Activity 5: History Record Book *(Offline)*

Activity 6. Optional: Create a Travel Brochure *(Offline)*

Activity 7. Optional: Athens: Democracy on the Aegean *(Offline)*

ASSESS

Lesson Assessment: Athens and Democracy (*Offline*)

You will complete an offline assessment covering the main objectives of this lesson. Your learning coach will score this assessment.

LEARN

Activity 8. Optional: Democracy at Work *(Offline)*

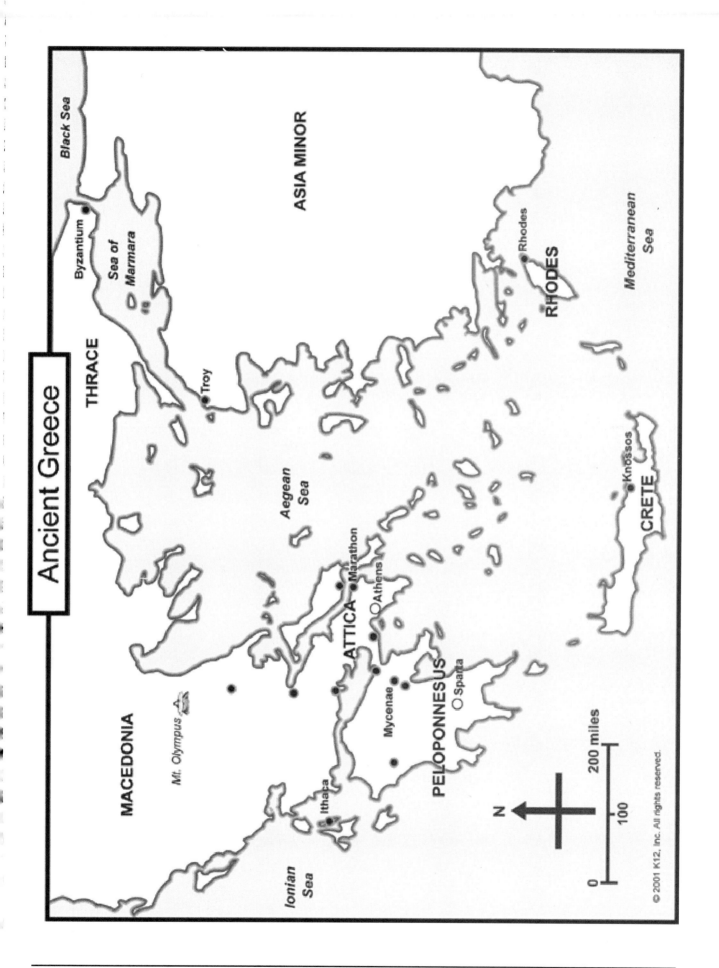

Ancient Greece

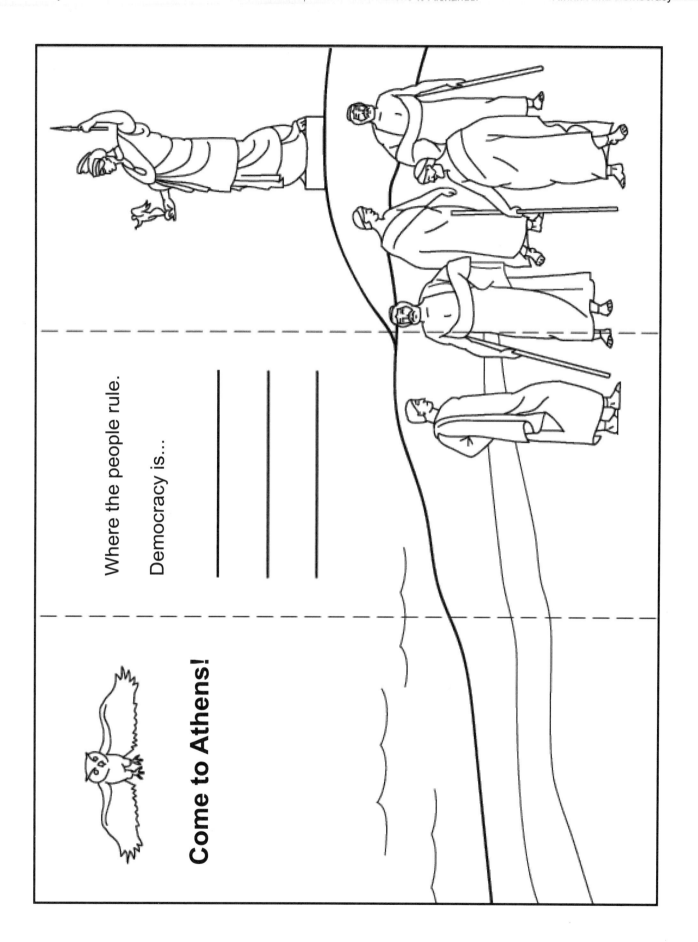

Where the people rule.

Democracy is...

_____

Come to Athens!

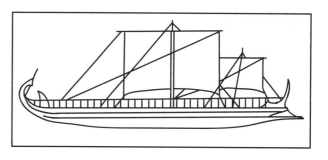

Name _____ Date _____

Lesson Assessment

Athens and Democracy

Use your map of Ancient Greece to answer question 1.

1. Where is Athens on your map?

2. What does the word *democracy* mean?

3. Was ancient Athens a democracy?

4. How did the people make those decisions about how to run the city?

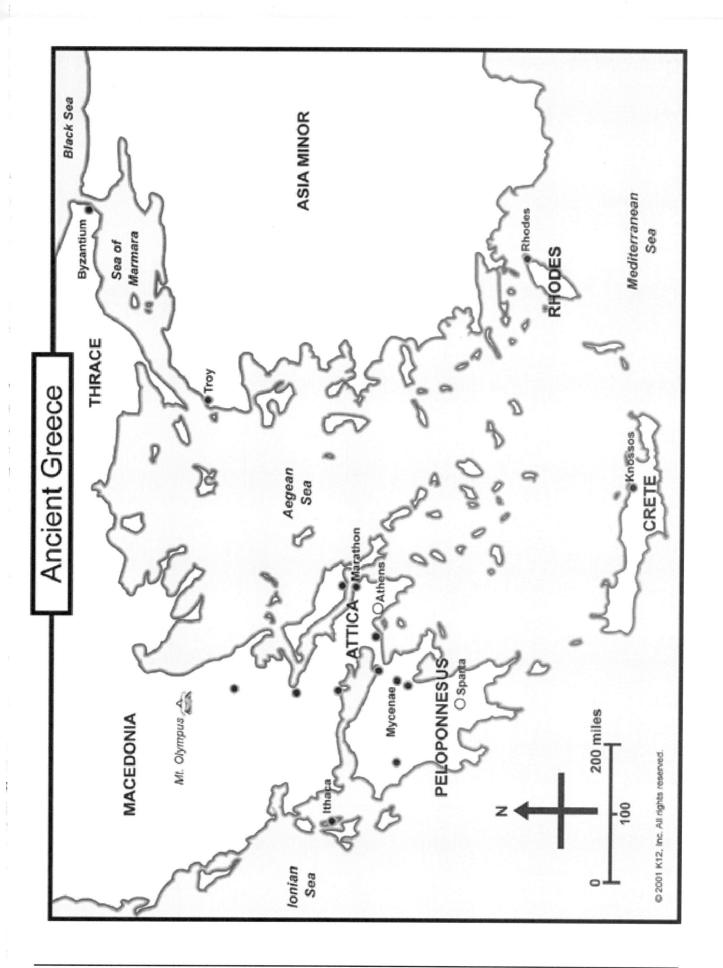

Ancient Greece

Black Sea

THRACE

MACEDONIA

Byzantium

Sea of
Marmara

ASIA MINOR

Troy

Mt. Olympus

Aegean
Sea

RHODES

Rhodes

Mediterranean
Sea

Ionian
Sea

Ithaca

ATTICA

Marathon
Athens

Mycenae

PELOPONNESUS

Sparta

Knossos

CRETE

N

0   100   200 miles

© 2001 K12, Inc. All rights reserved.

Student Guide
Lesson 3: Sparta: Be Brave and Strong

Each city-state in Greece had its own distinctive way of life. In Sparta, strength, endurance, and bravery in battle were valued above all else. The Spartans were a warrior people, known for their toughness and discipline.

Lesson Objectives

- Describe the Spartans as a warrior people.
- Explain that Spartans were known for their toughness and bravery.
- Locate Sparta on a map.

PREPARE

Approximate lesson time is 60 minutes.

Materials

For the Student

    📖 map of Ancient Greece

    crayons, 16 or more

    pencils, no. 2

    paper, 8 1/2" x 11"

    📖 Life of a Spartan Boy coloring sheet

    pencils, colored, 16 or more

    📖 Sparta: The Warrior City-State cut-out sheet

    glue sticks

    index cards, 4" x 6"

    scissors, round-end safety

Keywords and Pronunciation

Alexandros (ah-lek-SAHN-drohs)

Cassandra (kuh-SAN-druh)

Lykia (LIYK-yuh)

LEARN
Activity 1: It's Not Greek to Me *(Online)*

Activity 2: Sparta and Athens *(Online)*

Activity 3: Alexandros's Sparta *(Online)*

Activity 4: Sparta: Be Brave and Strong *(Online)*

Activity 5: History Record Book *(Offline)*

Activity 6. Optional: Life of a Spartan Boy *(Offline)*

Activity 7. Optional: Sparta: The Warrior City-State *(Offline)*

ASSESS

Lesson Assessment: Sparta: Be Brave and Strong *(Offline)*

You will complete an offline assessment covering the main objectives of this lesson. Your learning coach will score this assessment.

LEARN
Activity 8. Optional: A Spartan Life *(Offline)*

Ancient Greece

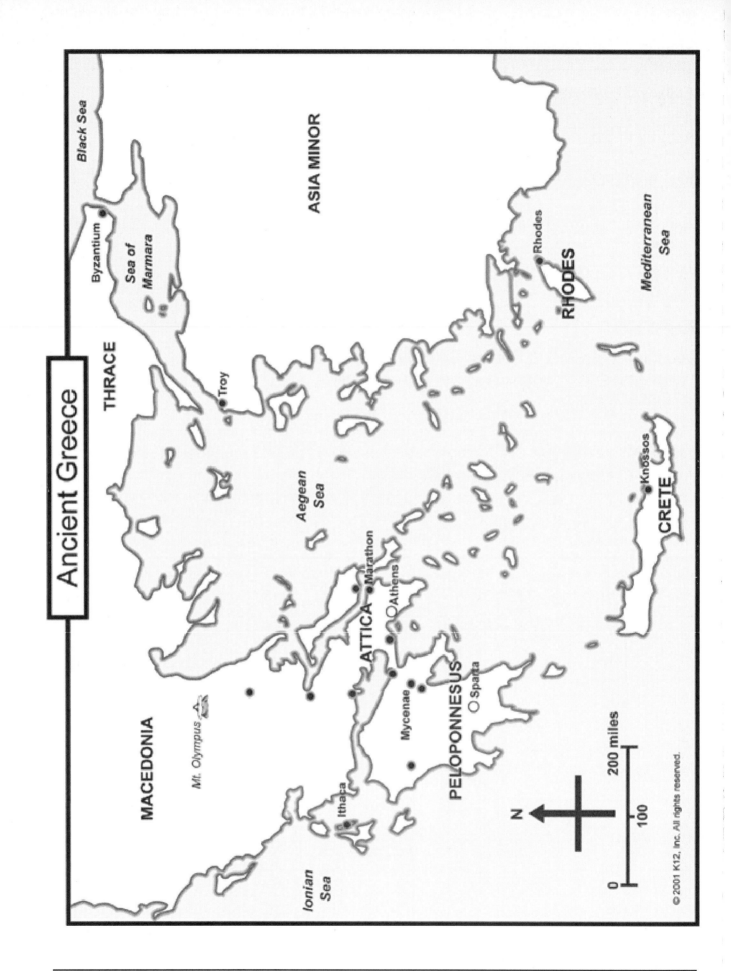

Black Sea

ASIA MINOR

Byzantium

Sea of Marmara

Rhodes

RHODES

Mediterranean Sea

THRACE

Troy

Aegean Sea

Knossos

CRETE

MACEDONIA

Mt. Olympus

Marathon

Athens

ATTICA

Mycenae

PELOPONNESUS

Sparta

Ithaca

Ionian Sea

N

0   100   200 miles

© 2001 K12, Inc. All rights reserved.

Name _____   Date _____

Life of a Spartan Boy

Complete the timeline by putting each symbol below into the corresponding box on the timeline.
Color the Spartan soldier.

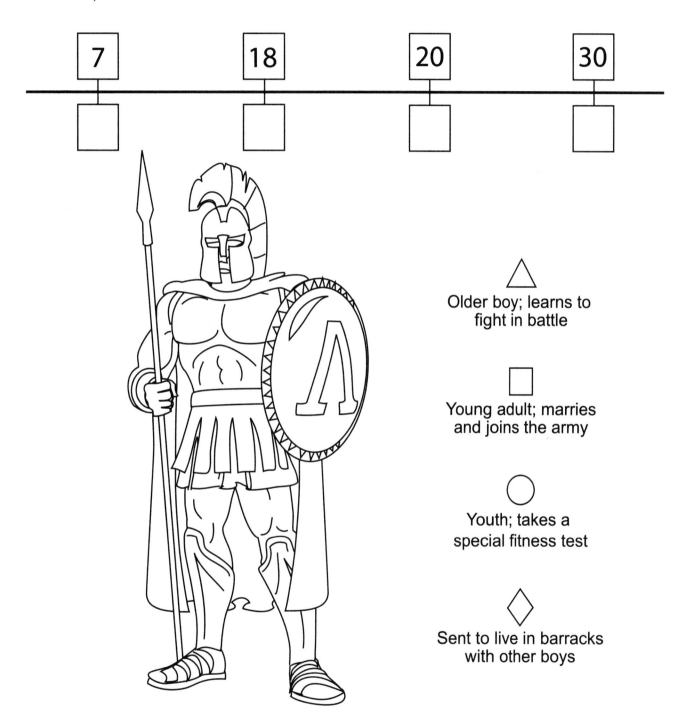

△
Older boy; learns to
fight in battle

□
Young adult; marries
and joins the army

○
Youth; takes a
special fitness test

◇
Sent to live in barracks
with other boys

cut

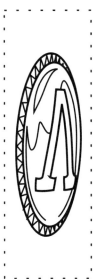

Lesson Assessment

Sparta: Be Brave and Strong

Use your map of Ancient Greece to answer question 1.

1. Where is Sparta on your map?

2. Would you describe Spartans as farmers, artists, or great warriors?

3. What were Spartans known for?

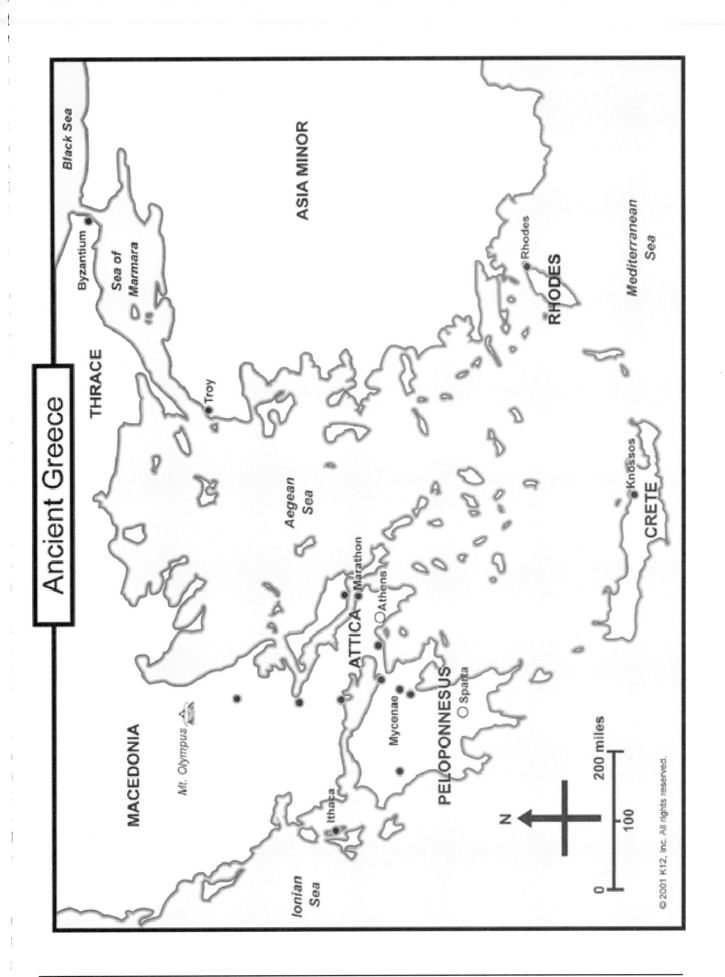

Ancient Greece

THRACE

Black Sea

Byzantium

Sea of Marmara

ASIA MINOR

Troy

MACEDONIA

Mt. Olympus

Aegean Sea

Rhodes

RHODES

Mediterranean Sea

Knossos

CRETE

ATTICA

Marathon

Athens

PELOPONNESUS

Mycenae

Sparta

Ithaca

Ionian Sea

N

0   100   200 miles

© 2001 K12, Inc. All rights reserved.

Student Guide
Lesson 4: Persia Rising: Darius on the Move

Lesson Objectives

- Name Darius as an emperor who ruled the Persian Empire.
- Explain that the Athenians fought against Emperor Darius.
- Locate the Persian Empire on a map.

PREPARE

Approximate lesson time is 60 minutes.

Materials

For the Student

    📖 map of the Persian Empire

    crayons, 16 or more

    pencils, no. 2

    pencils, colored, 16 or more

    📖 Behistun Rock activity sheet

    paper, 8 1/2" x 11"

    Courage, Esther! by Carolyn Nystrom

Keywords and Pronunciation

Darius (duh-RIY-uhs)

satrap (SAY-trap)

LEARN
Activity 1: Sparta and Athens *(Online)*

Activity 2: Mighty King of a Mighty Empire *(Online)*

Activity 3: Persia Rising: Darius on the Move *(Online)*

Activity 4: History Record Book *(Offline)*

Activity 5. Optional: Behistun Rock *(Offline)*

Activity 6. Optional: The Greek Rebels *(Offline)*

ASSESS
Lesson Assessment: Persia Rising: Darius on the Move (*Offline*)
You will complete an offline assessment covering the main objectives of this lesson. Your learning coach will score this assessment.

LEARN
Activity 7. Optional: Esther, Queen of Persia *(Offline)*

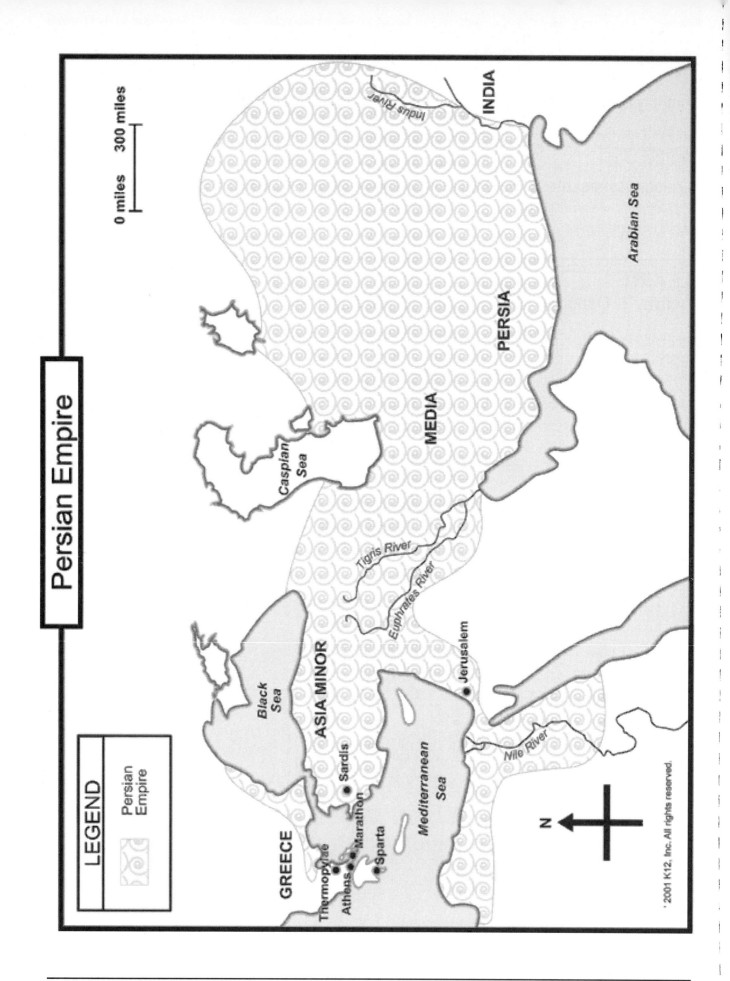

Persian Empire

LEGEND

Persian Empire

0 miles — 300 miles

INDIA

Indus River

Arabian Sea

PERSIA

MEDIA

Caspian Sea

Tigris River

Euphrates River

Jerusalem

ASIA MINOR

Black Sea

Sardis

Marathon

Mediterranean Sea

Nile River

Thermopylae

Athens

Sparta

GREECE

N

© 2001 K12, Inc. All rights reserved.

Name   Date

The Behistun Rock

What would you want to say about Emperor Darius? On the lines below, write a
sentence or two about this mighty emperor of Persia. Imagine that your words will be engraved on
the Behistun Rock.

_____

_____

_____

_____

Name _____ Date _____

Lesson Assessment

Persia Rising: Darius on the Move

Use your map of the Persian Empire to answer question 1.

1. Where is Persian Empire located?

2. Who ruled the Persian Empire?

3. Who came to help the Greeks who were rebelling against Darius?

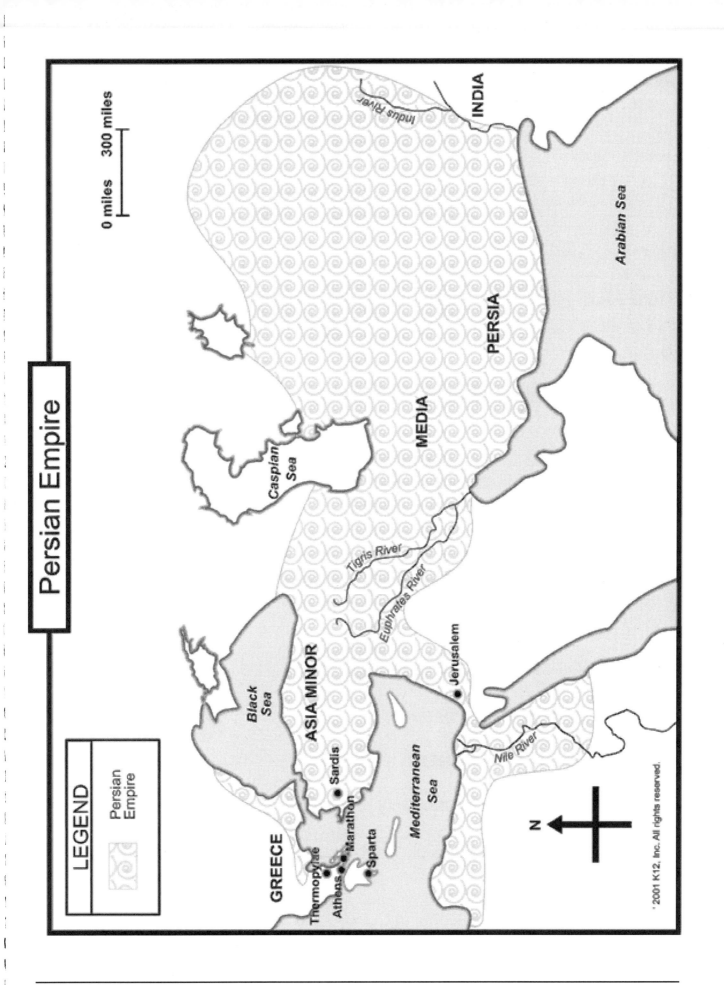

Persian Empire

LEGEND

Persian Empire

0 miles 300 miles

GREECE
Thermopylae
Athens
Marathon
Sparta
Sardis
ASIA MINOR
Black Sea
Caspian Sea
Mediterranean Sea
Jerusalem
Nile River
Tigris River
Euphrates River
MEDIA
PERSIA
Arabian Sea
INDIA
Indus River

N

Student Guide
Lesson 5: The Battle of Marathon

Lesson Objectives

- Explain that the Persians tried to conquer Greece.
- Explain that the Greeks defeated the Persians at Marathon.
- Retell the story of the messenger who ran from Marathon to Athens with news of the Athenian victory over the Persians.

PREPARE

Approximate lesson time is 60 minutes.

Materials

For the Student

    📭 map of the Persian Empire

    crayons, 16 or more

    pencils, no. 2

    paper, 8 1/2" x 11"

    📭 From Marathon to Athens activity sheet

    📭 Retelling the Battle of Marathon activity sheet

LEARN
Activity 1: Looking Back *(Online)*

Activity 2: The Battle of Marathon *(Online)*

Activity 3: The Battle of Marathon *(Online)*

Activity 4: History Record Book *(Offline)*

Activity 5. Optional: From Marathon to Athens *(Offline)*

Activity 6. Optional: Retelling the Story of the Battle of Marathon *(Offline)*

ASSESS

Lesson Assessment: The Battle of Marathon (*Offline*)

You will complete an offline assessment covering the main objectives of this lesson. Your learning coach will score this assessment.

LEARN

Activity 7. Optional: A Modern Marathon (*Offline*)

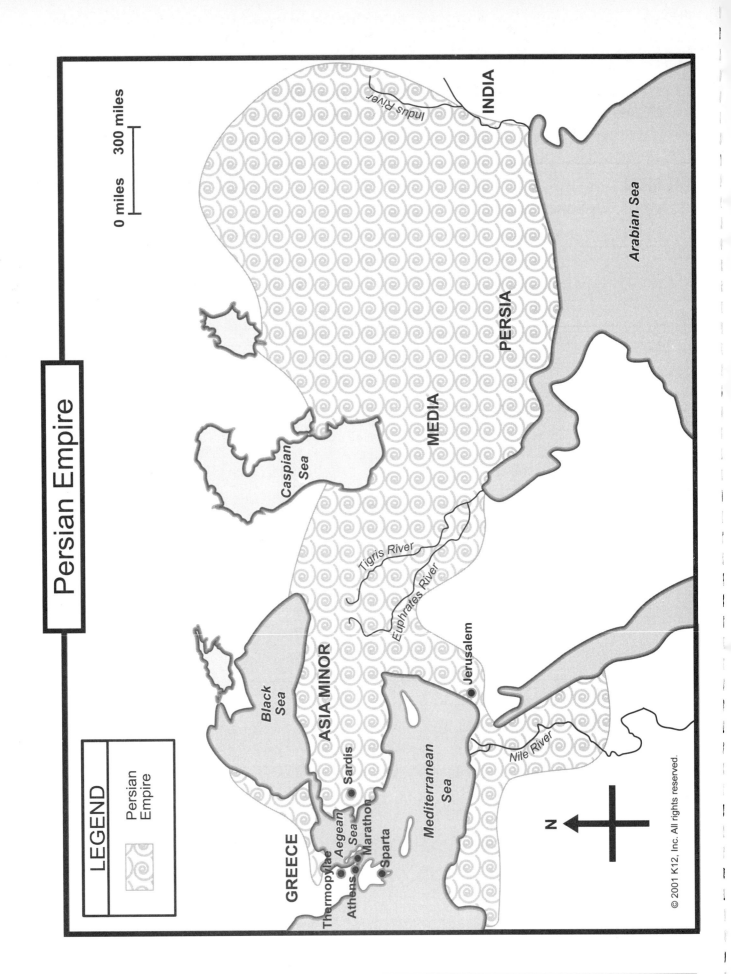

Persian Empire

LEGEND

Persian Empire

0 miles

300 miles

GREECE
Thermopylae
Athens
Aegean Sea
Marathon
Sparta

Black Sea

ASIA MINOR
Sardis

Mediterranean Sea

Caspian Sea

Tigris River

Euphrates River

Jerusalem

Nile River

MEDIA

PERSIA

Indus River

INDIA

Arabian Sea

N

From Marathon to Athens

Select the correct information from the boxes below the Marathon runner. Cut it out and glue it in the thought bubble above the runner's head.

The Romans attacked but we defeated them.

The Persians attacked and defeated us.

The Persians attacked but we defeated them.

Retelling the Story of the Battle of Marathon

Cut out each picture showing a scene from the Battle of Marathon. Arrange them in the order in which they occurred. Glue them on the sheet. Write, or dictate, one or two sentences describing what's going on in the picture. Then start at the beginning and retell the story of the Battle of Marathon in your own words.

Name _____   Date _____

Lesson Assessment

The Battle of Marathon

1. Emperor Darius was angry with the Athenians because they had sent some soldiers to fight against him. How did he try to get revenge?

2. What two armies fought in the Battle of Marathon?

3. Who won the Battle of Marathon?

4. After the the Battle of Marathon, how did the news travel to Athens?

Student Guide
Lesson 6: The Battle of Thermopylae

Lesson Objectives

- Name the Greeks and the Persians as the two forces that fought each other at the Battle of Thermopylae.
- Explain that the Greeks lost the Battle of Thermopylae, but the delay allowed the Athenians to get their navy ready.
- State that the Greeks won the war against the Persians.

PREPARE

Approximate lesson time is 60 minutes.

Materials

For the Student

📇 map of the Persian Empire

crayons, 16 or more

pencils, no. 2

paper, 8 1/2" x 11"

📇 The Battle of Thermopylae coloring sheet

📇 Herald's Message activity sheet

Keywords and Pronunciation

Leonidas (lee-AHN-uh-duhs)

Salamis (SA-luh-muhs)

Thermopylae (thuhr-MAH-puh-lee)

LEARN
Activity 1: Review the Battle of Marathon *(Online)*

Activity 2: Thermopylae *(Online)*

Activity 3: The Battle of Thermopylae *(Online)*

Activity 4: History Record Book *(Offline)*

Activity 5. Optional: Battle at Thermopylae (Offline)

Activity 6. Optional: Herald's Message (Offline)

ASSESS

Lesson Assessment: The Battle of Thermopylae (Offline)

You will complete an offline assessment covering the main objectives of this lesson. Your learning coach will score this assessment.

LEARN

Activity 7. Optional: Why the Spartans? (Online)

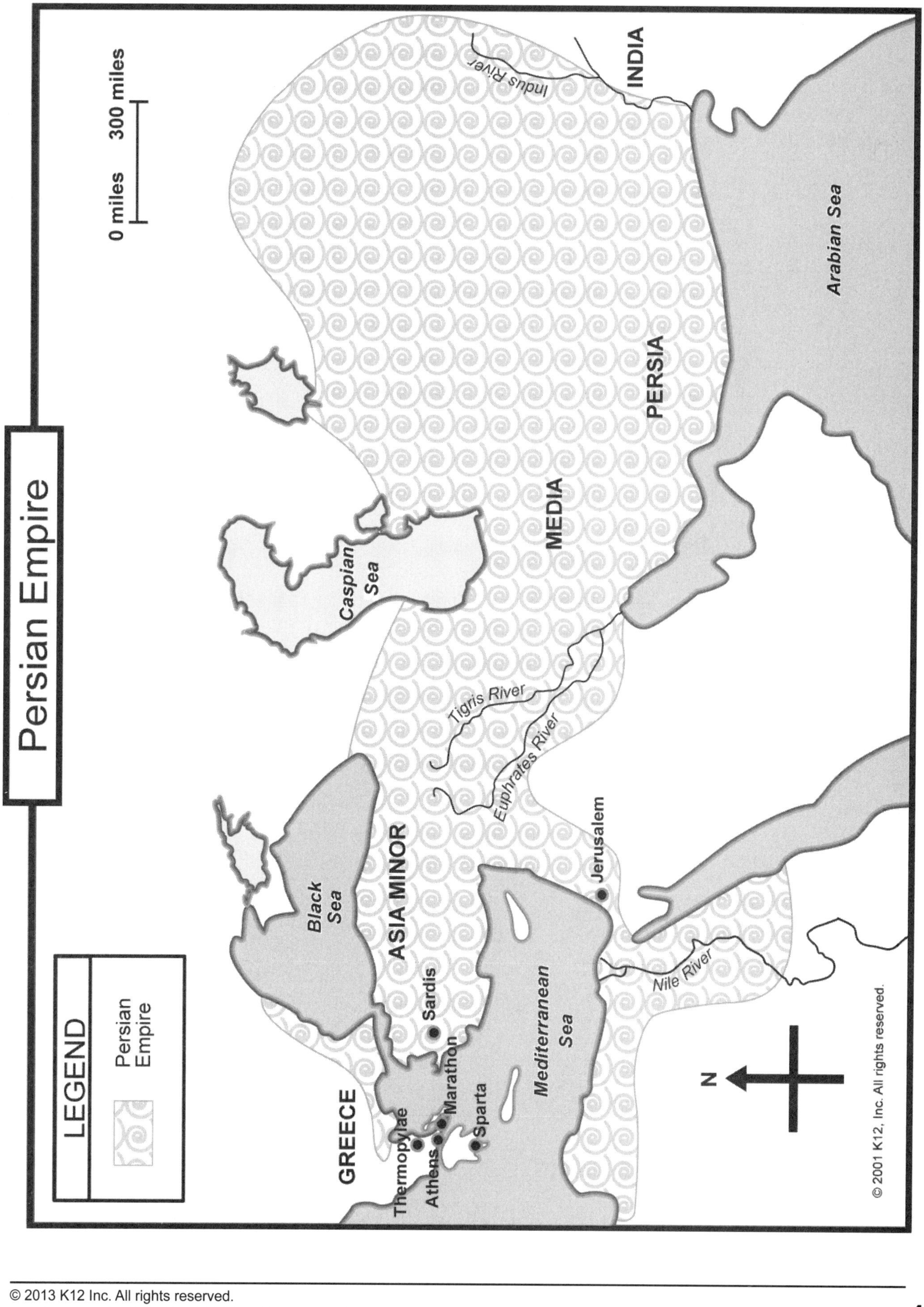
Persian Empire
LEGEND
Persian Empire
0 miles
300 miles
N
INDIA
Indus River
Arabian Sea
PERSIA
MEDIA
Caspian Sea
Tigris River
Euphrates River
Jerusalem
ASIA MINOR
Black Sea
Sardis
Mediterranean Sea
Nile River
GREECE
Thermopylae
Athens
Marathon
Sparta
© 2001 K12, Inc. All rights reserved.

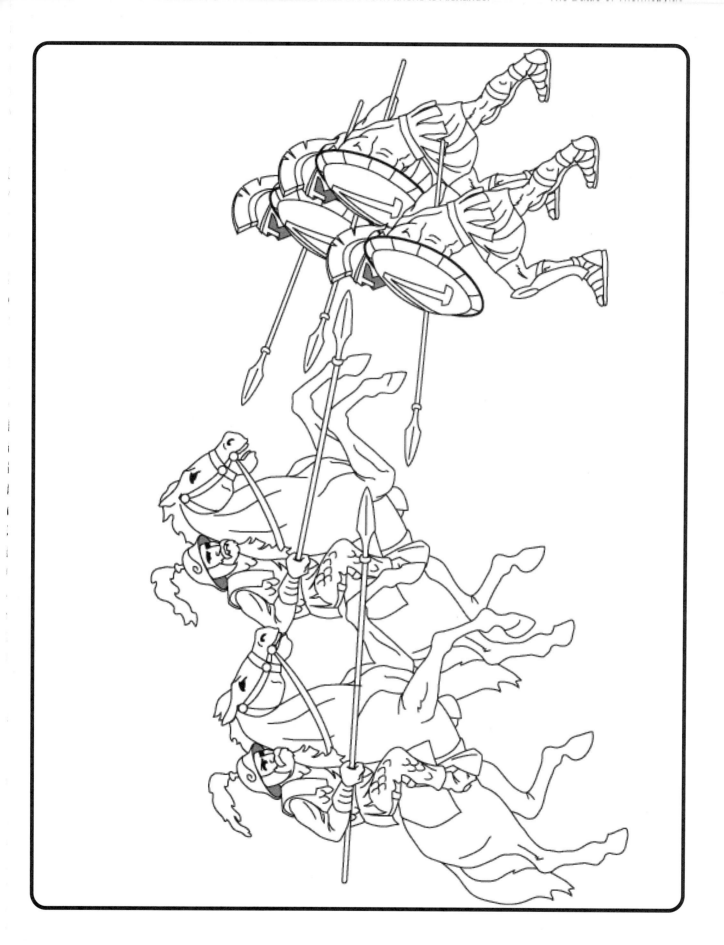

Name _____   Date _____

The Herald's Message

Fill in each blank with the correct word. Use the word bank at the bottom of the scroll. Practice reading the announcement, then pretend you are the herald and read aloud the news about the battle at Thermopylae.

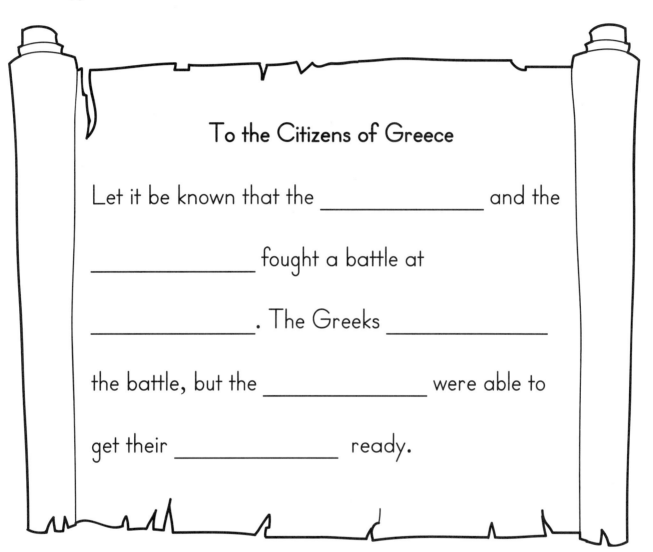

To the Citizens of Greece

Let it be known that the _____ and the

_____ fought a battle at

_____. The Greeks _____

the battle, but the _____ were able to

get their _____ ready.

Word Bank

Thermopylae	navy	Persians	lost	Athenians	Greeks

Name _____   Date _____

Lesson Assessment

The Battle of Thermopylae

1. Which two armies fought a famous battle at a place called Thermopylae?

2. Even though the Greeks lost the battle at Thermopylae, the soldiers who fought there saved Greece. How?

3. Who won the Persian Wars, the Greeks or the Persians?

Student Guide
Lesson 7: The Golden Age of Athens: Pericles

Lesson Objectives

- Identify Pericles as a leader of Athens.
- Explain that Pericles believed in democracy and helped turn Athens into one of the greatest cities in the world.
- Identify the Parthenon from a picture.
- Tell that the Parthenon, a temple in Athens, was dedicated to Athena.

PREPARE

Approximate lesson time is 60 minutes.

Materials

For the Student

    🖳 map of the Persian Empire

    map, world

    pencils, no. 2

    paper, 8 1/2" x 11"

    pencils, colored, 16 or more

    🖳 Pericles coloring sheet

    crayons, 16 or more

    🖳 Parthenon coloring sheet

    clay, colored

    rolling pin

    paper, wax

Keywords and Pronunciation

Acropolis (uh-KRAH-puh-luhs)

frieze (freez)

Parthenon (PAHR-thuh-nahn)

Pericles (PEHR-uh-kleez)

LEARN
Activity 1: A Quick Review *(Online)*

Activity 2: Pericles: Leader of Athens *(Online)*

Activity 3: A Golden Age *(Online)*

Activity 4: The Golden Age of Athens: Pericles *(Online)*

Activity 5: History Record Book *(Offline)*

Activity 6. Optional: Pericles *(Offline)*

Activity 7. Optional: The Parthenon *(Offline)*

ASSESS

Lesson Assessment: The Golden Age of Athens: Pericles (*Online*)

You will complete an offline assessment covering the main objectives of this lesson. Your learning coach will score this assessment.

LEARN
Activity 8. Optional: Make a Frieze *(Offline)*

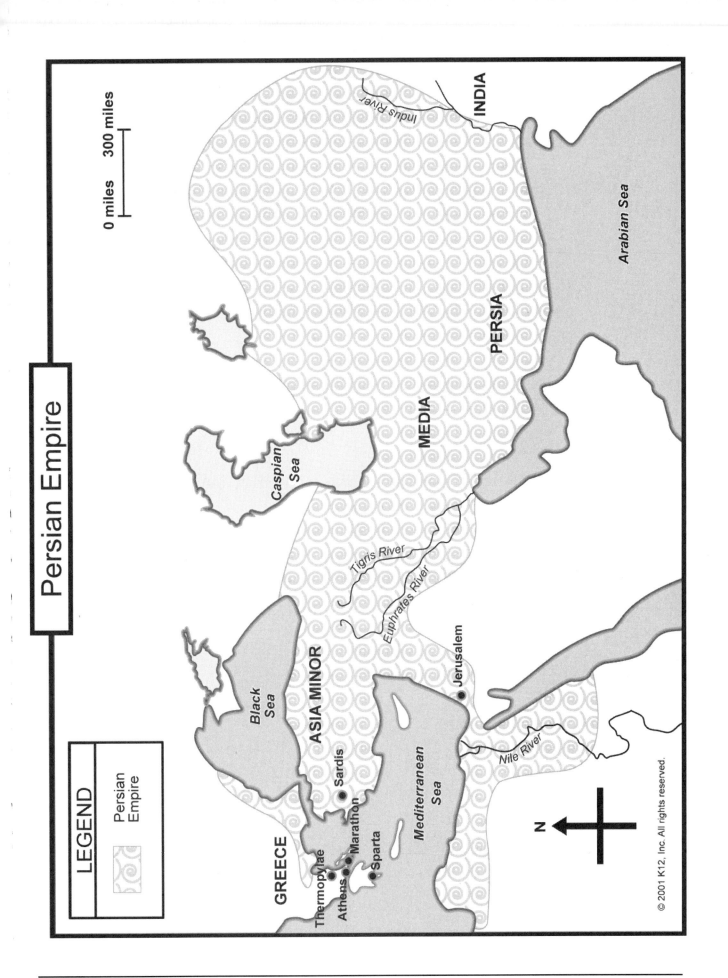

Persian Empire

LEGEND

Persian Empire

0 miles — 300 miles

INDIA

Indus River

Arabian Sea

PERSIA

MEDIA

Caspian Sea

Tigris River

Euphrates River

Jerusalem

Nile River

Black Sea

ASIA MINOR

Sardis

Mediterranean Sea

Marathon

Sparta

Thermopylae

Athens

GREECE

N

Name _____ Date _____

_____ — Leader of Athens

Name

Date

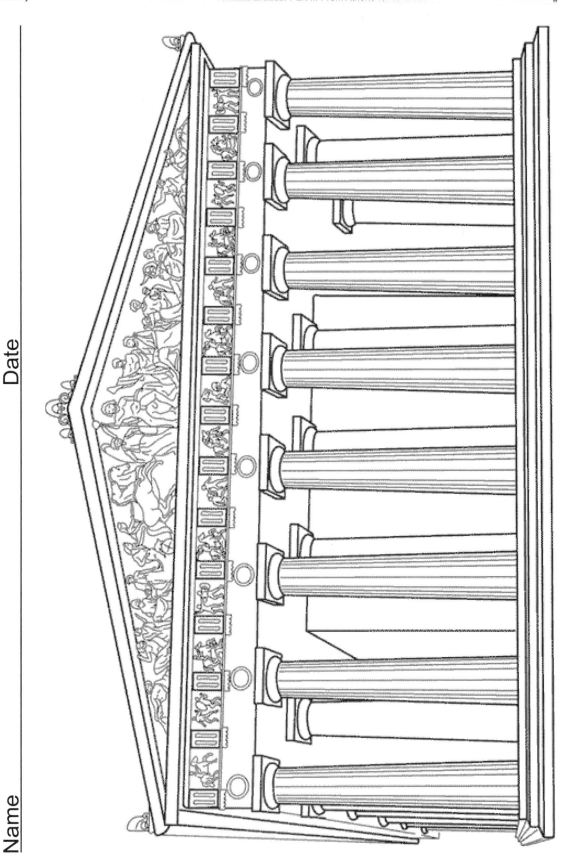

Parthenon: Temple Dedicated to _____

Name _____ Date _____

Lesson Assessment

The Golden Age of Athens: Pericles

1. What was the name of the leader who helped rebuild Athens after the war with Persia?

2. What did Pericles believe in?

3. Which image shows the Parthenon?

   A.

   B.

   C.

4. Who was the Parthenon dedicated to?

Student Guide
Lesson 8: Lovers of Wisdom

Lesson Objectives

- Define philosopher as a thinker or a person who loves wisdom.
- Identify Socrates, Plato, and Aristotle as philosophers from Athens.

PREPARE

Approximate lesson time is 60 minutes.

Materials

For the Student

📖 map of the Persian Empire

pencils, no. 2

paper, 8 1/2" x 11"

pencils, colored, 16 or more

📖 Philosophers Think activity sheet

crayons, 16 or more

📖 Philosophers from Athens activity sheet

markers, colored, 8 or more

Keywords and Pronunciation

agora (A-guh-ruh)
Aristotle (AIR-uh-stah-tl)
Plato (PLAY-toh)
Socrates (SAHK-ruh-teez)

LEARN
Activity 1: Question and Answer *(Online)*

Activity 2: Philosophers of Athens *(Online)*

Activity 3: Lovers of Wisdom *(Online)*

Activity 4: History Record Book *(Offline)*

Activity 5. Optional: Philosophers Think *(Offline)*

Activity 6. Optional: Philosophers from Athens *(Offline)*

ASSESS
Lesson Assessment: Lovers of Wisdom (*Offline*)
You will complete an offline assessment covering the main objectives of this lesson. Your learning coach will score this assessment.

LEARN
Activity 7. Optional: More Thinking *(Offline)*

Persian Empire

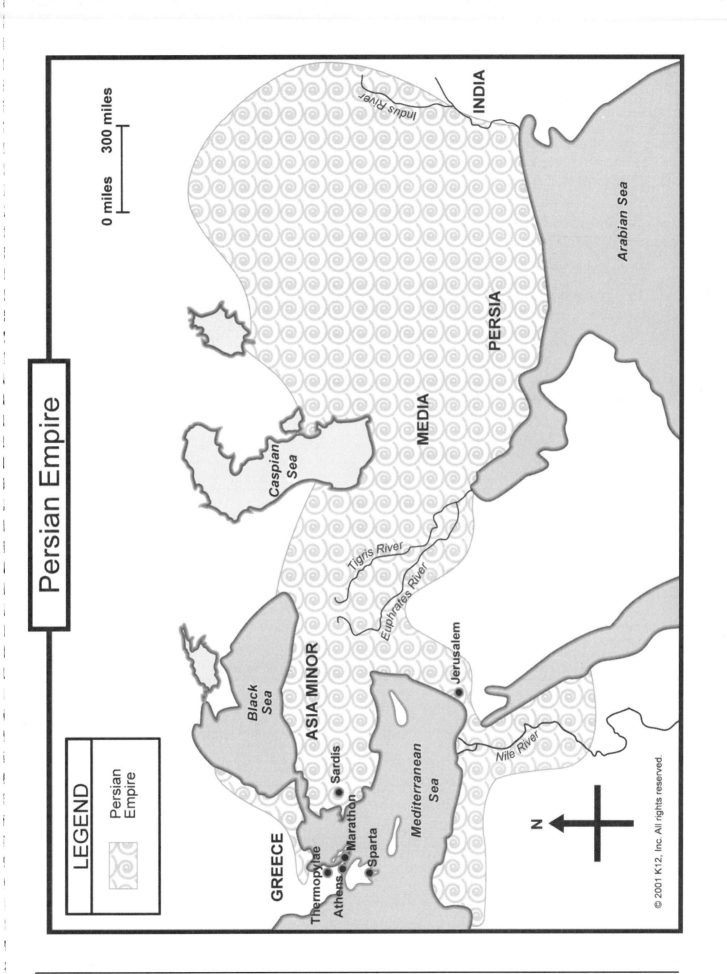

LEGEND

Persian Empire

0 miles 300 miles

GREECE
Thermopylae
Athens
Marathon
Sparta
Sardis
ASIA MINOR
Black Sea
Mediterranean Sea
Jerusalem
Nile River
Caspian Sea
Tigris River
Euphrates River
MEDIA
PERSIA
INDIA
Indus River
Arabian Sea

N

145

Name _____   Date _____

Philosophers Think

Socrates, Plato, and Aristotle liked to think. They had many questions they wanted to answer. Here are some questions they may have thought about. Which of these would you like to think about? Use a crayon to circle the three questions that interest you the most. Then think of another question of your own. Write it at the bottom.

Aristotle

Socrates

Plato

Why do we have day and night?

Why can't people breathe underwater?

Why is some water salty?

Why can't animals talk to people?

Why do we need food?

Why are there rules?

Why do people look different?

Why are there so many different animals?

Why can't people fly?

Why are there so many different languages?

_____

_____

_____

_____

Name _____   Date _____

Philosophers from Athens

Socrates, Plato, and Aristotle were three of the most famous Greek philosophers. People made sculptures of them. Use a black marker or crayon to trace the outline of their faces. Then use three other colors to trace their names.

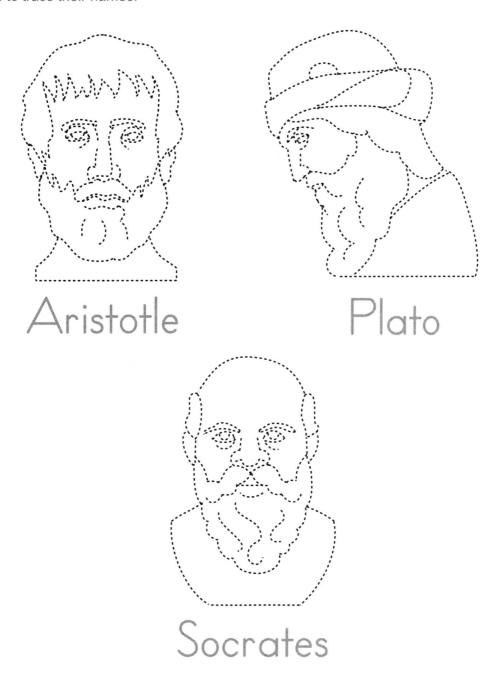

Aristotle

Plato

Socrates

Lesson Assessment

Lovers of Wisdom

1. What's the long word we use to describe someone who loves learning and wisdom?

2. We learned about three very famous men who spent their time thinking big thoughts, trying to figure things out, and teaching others. What were their names?

Student Guide
Lesson 9. Optional: The Greeks Fight Each Other: The Peloponnesian War

The city-states of Athens and Sparta fought together against the mighty Persian Empire and won the Persian Wars. But then Athens and Sparta fought each other in a terrible war that lasted twenty-seven years: the Peloponnesian War.

Lesson Objectives

- Name Athens and Sparta as the Greek city-states that fought the long Peloponnesian War.
- Explain that fighting the Peloponnesian War weakened all of the Greek city-states.
- Identify Sparta as the winner of the Peloponnesian War.

PREPARE

Approximate lesson time is 60 minutes.

Materials

For the Student

📖 map of Classical Greece

pencils, no. 2

paper, 8 1/2" x 11"

pencils, colored, 16 or more

📖 Greeks at War activity sheet

crayons, 16 or more

paper, colored construction, 12"x12"

Elmer's Glue-All

scissors, round-end safety

📖 Athens Versus Sparta activity sheet

Keywords and Pronunciation

Hellespont (HEH-luh-spahnt)

Peloponnesian (peh-luh-puh-NEE-zhuhn)

Peloponnesus (peh-luh-puh-NEE-suhs)

LEARN

Activity 1. Optional: Optional Lesson Instructions (Online)

This lesson is OPTIONAL. It is provided for students who seek enrichment or extra practice. You may skip this lesson.

If you choose to skip this lesson, then go to the Plan or Lesson Lists page and mark this lesson "Skipped" in order to proceed to the next lesson in the course.

Activity 2. Optional: Question and Answer *(Online)*

Activity 3. Optional: The Peloponnesian War Begins *(Online)*

Activity 4. Optional: The War Continues *(Online)*

Activity 5. Optional: The War Ends *(Online)*

Activity 6. Optional: The Greeks Fight Each Other: The Peloponnesian War *(Online)*

Activity 7. Optional: History Record Book *(Offline)*

Activity 8. Optional: The Greeks at War *(Offline)*

Activity 9. Optional: Athens Versus Sparta *(Offline)*

Activity 10. Optional: More About the Peloponnesian War *(Online)*

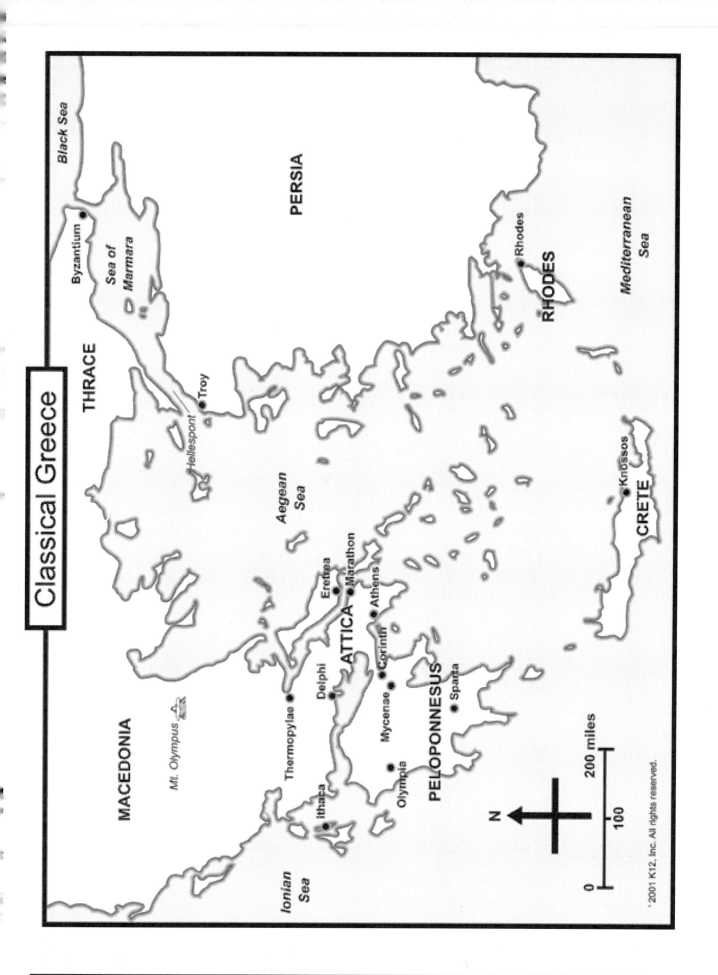

Classical Greece

Greeks at War

Color the pictures. Cut them out. Glue them in order. Talk about the long Peloponnesian War.

 cut

Athens sends its ships to conquer other city-states.

Athenian farmers move inside the walls of Athens.

Sparta decides to fight Athens.

Sparta wins.

Spartans attack Athenian ships at the Hellespont and defeat Athenian solders.

Name _____   Date _____

Greeks at War

Use three different-colored crayons to mark the pictures with the following letters to show what
Athens and Sparta did during the Peloponnesian War. A=Athens, S=Sparta, AS=Athens and Sparta

1_____

2_____

3_____

4_____

Student Guide
Lesson 10: Young Alexander

Lesson Objectives

- Tell that the king of Macedonia conquered the Greek city-states.
- State that Bucephalus was Alexander's horse.
- Tell major events of the story of the Gordian Knot.

PREPARE

Approximate lesson time is 60 minutes.

Materials

For the Student

📖 map of Classical Greece

pencils, no. 2

paper, 8 1/2" x 11"

pencils, colored, 16 or more

📖 Who Was Alexander's Horse? activity sheet

crayons, 16 or more

📖 The Story of the Gordian Knot activity sheet

glue sticks

paper, colored construction, 12"x12"

scissors, round-end safety

Keywords and Pronunciation

Achilles (uh-KIH-leez)
Bucephalus (byoo-SEH-fuh-luhs)
Gordian (GOR-dee-uhn)
Macedon (MA-suh-dahn)
Macedonia (ma-suh-DOH-nee-uh)
Macedonian (ma-suh-DOH-nee-uhn)

LEARN
Activity 1: Question and Answer *(Online)*

Activity 2: The Young Man with Big Dreams *(Online)*

Activity 3: Young Alexander *(Online)*

Activity 4: History Record Book *(Offline)*

Activity 5. Optional: Who Was Alexander's Horse? *(Offline)*

Activity 6. Optional: The Story of the Gordian Knot *(Offline)*

ASSESS

Lesson Assessment: Young Alexander (*Offline*)

You will complete an offline assessment covering the main objectives of this lesson. Your learning coach will score this assessment.

LEARN

Activity 7. Optional: Learn More About Alexander *(Online)*

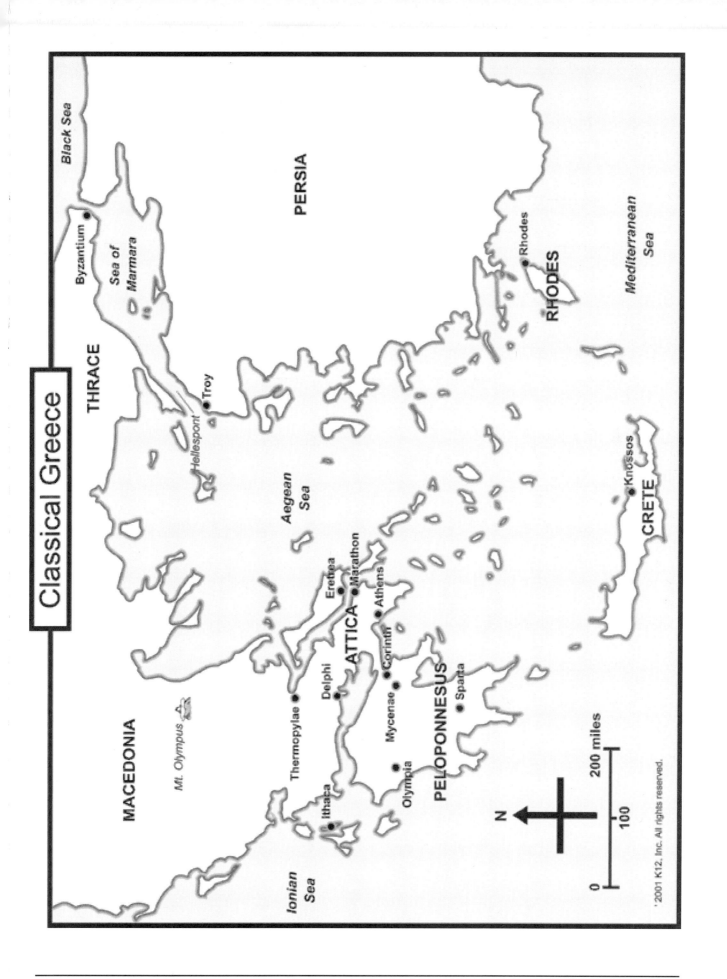

Classical Greece

Black Sea

THRACE

Byzantium

Sea of Marmara

PERSIA

Troy

Hellespont

RHODES

Rhodes

Mediterranean Sea

MACEDONIA

Mt. Olympus

Aegean Sea

Thermopylae

Delphi

Eretrea

Marathon

ATTICA

Athens

Corinth

Ithaca

Mycenae

Olympia

PELOPONNESUS

Sparta

Knossos

CRETE

Ionian Sea

N

200 miles

100

0

©2001 K12, Inc. All rights reserved.

Name _____   Date _____

Who Was Alexander's Horse?

Color this picture of a famous statue of Alexander the Great and his horse, Bucephalus. Then write the horse's name under the picture. Then read the sentences about his horse. Cross out the ones that are NOT true.

1. Bucephalus was afraid of his own shadow.
2. Alexander's father could ride Bucephalus.
3. Bucephalus was a coal-black horse.
4. It was easy for Alexander to ride Bucephalus.
5. Bucephalus and Alexander stayed together for many years.

The Story of the Gordian Knot

Tell the story of the Gordian Knot. Cut out the sentences and glue them to the pictures they describe. Then color the pictures. Next, cut them out and glue them in the correct order on a piece of construction paper.

 cut

Alexander becomes king.	Alexander cuts the Gordian Knot.
Alexander goes to the city.	Alexander hopes to rule the whole world.

165

Name _____   Date _____

Lesson Assessment

Young Alexander

1. Who conquered the Greek city-states?

2. Who was Bucephalus?

3. It is said that Alexander once visited a city where he saw a large knot of rope called the Gordian Knot. What did the people who lived there tell Alexander about the Gordian Knot?

4. How did Alexander undo the Gordian Knot?

5. When Alexander undid the Gordian Knot, what did it show about him?

Student Guide
Lesson 11: Alexander the Great

Lesson Objectives

- Demonstrate mastery of important knowledge and skills taught in this unit.
- Explain that Alexander conquered many lands and created a vast empire.
- Explain that Alexander came to be known as "Alexander the Great."
- Identify Socrates, Plato, and Aristotle as philosophers from Athens.
- Identify Athena as the ancient Greek goddess of wisdom.
- Define democracy as the people rule.
- Describe ancient Athens as a democracy.
- Describe the Spartans as a warrior people.
- Explain that Spartans were known for their toughness and bravery.
- Explain that the Greeks defeated the Persians at Marathon.
- Retell the story of the messenger who ran from Marathon to Athens with news of the Athenian victory over the Persians.
- Identify the Parthenon from a picture.

PREPARE

Approximate lesson time is 60 minutes.

Materials

For the Student

- map of Alexander's Empire
- Alexander's Empire activity sheet

   crayons, 16 or more

   clay, colored

   History Record Book

Keywords and Pronunciation

Bucephala (byoo-SEH-fuh-luh)

LEARN
Activity 1: A Quick Review *(Online)*

Activity 2: No More Worlds to Conquer *(Online)*

Activity 3: Where Did Alexander Go? *(Online)*

Activity 4: Did Alexander Conquer the World? *(Online)*

Activity 5. Optional: Alexander's World *(Offline)*

Activity 6. Optional: Alexander Looks Great! *(Offline)*

Activity 7: Reviewing Unit Six *(Online)*

ASSESS

Unit Assessment: Ancient Greece, Part II: From Athens to Alexander (*Offline*)

Complete an offline Unit Assessment. Your learning coach will score this part of the Assessment.

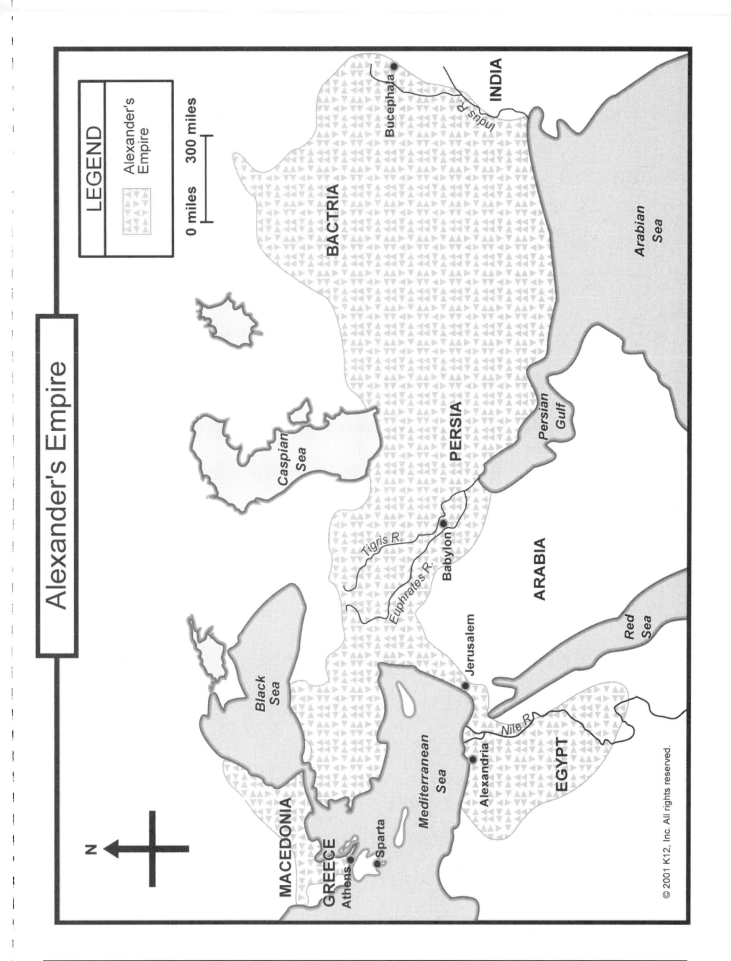

Alexander's Empire

LEGEND

Alexander's Empire

0 miles   300 miles

INDIA

Indus R.

Bucephala

BACTRIA

Arabian
Sea

PERSIA

Caspian
Sea

Persian
Gulf

Tigris R.

Euphrates R.

Babylon

ARABIA

Jerusalem

Red
Sea

Black
Sea

Nile R.

MACEDONIA

Alexandria

Mediterranean
Sea

EGYPT

N

GREECE

Athens

Sparta

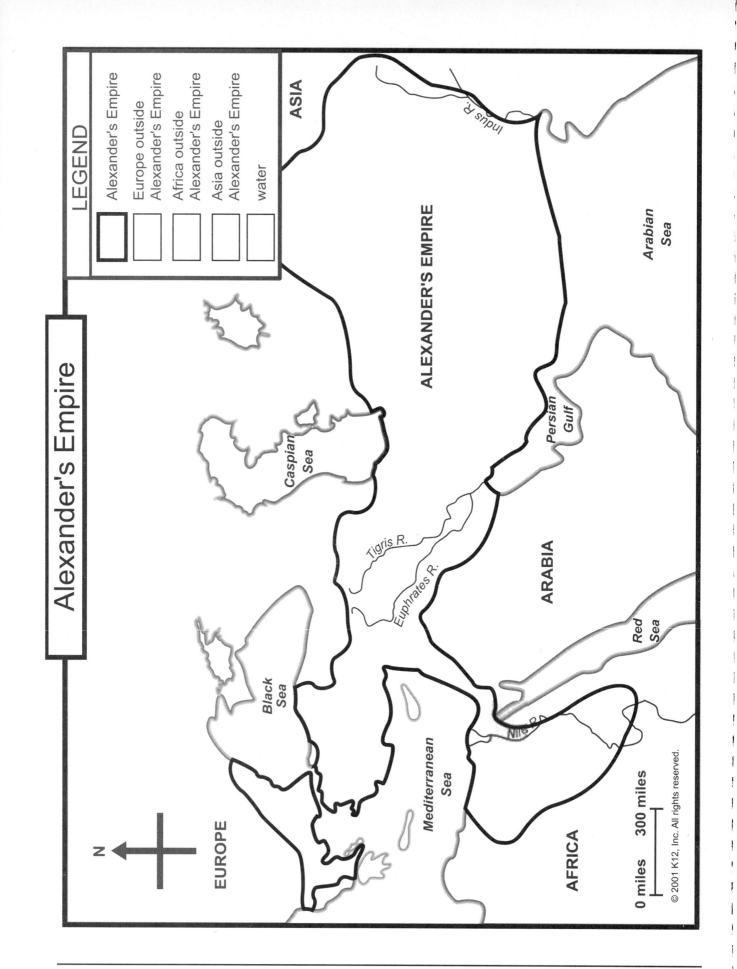

Alexander's Empire

LEGEND
- [ ] Alexander's Empire
- [ ] Europe outside Alexander's Empire
- [ ] Africa outside Alexander's Empire
- [ ] Asia outside Alexander's Empire
- [ ] water

ASIA

Indus R.

ALEXANDER'S EMPIRE

Arabian Sea

Caspian Sea

Persian Gulf

Tigris R.

Euphrates R.

ARABIA

Red Sea

Black Sea

Nile R.

Mediterranean Sea

EUROPE

N

AFRICA

0 miles   300 miles

© 2001 K12, Inc. All rights reserved.

Name _____   Date _____

Ancient Greece, Part II: From Athens to Alexander

Select the one best answer. Shade or color the bubble for the answer you choose.

1. Who was the ancient Greek goddess of wisdom?
   - ○ Pericles
   - ○ Athena
   - ○ Arachne

2. What does democracy mean?
   - ○ the kings rule
   - ○ the people rule
   - ○ the soldiers rule

3. Who were Socrates, Plato, and Aristotle?
   - ○ philosophers from Athens
   - ○ soldiers from Sparta
   - ○ senators from Rome

4. In which Greek city-state would you be more likely to find young boys training to become tough soldiers?
   - ○ Athens
   - ○ Sparta

5. The Greeks fought a famous battle against the Persians, and then sent a runner to Athens to announce their victory. Today, athletes sometimes run a long race in memory of that battle and brave messenger. What was the name of the battle?
   - ○ Thermopylae
   - ○ Marathon
   - ○ Olympus

6. What were the Spartans known for?

     ○ toughness and bravery

     ○ wisdom and kindness

     ○ books and poems

7. How would you describe ancient Athens?

     ○ It was ruled by kings.

     ○ It was run by the Persians.

     ○ It was a democracy.

8. Whom did the Greeks fight a war against and win?

     ○ the Macedonians

     ○ the Persians

     ○ the Romans

9. What did Alexander the Great do?

     ○ created a large empire by conquering many lands

     ○ ran a long distance with a message about the Battle of Marathon

     ○ fought against Darius at the Battle of Thermopylae

10. Look at these pictures. Draw a circle around the Parthenon.

Student Guide
Lesson 1: The Mystery of Mohenjo-Daro

Journey to the lands of ancient India, and explore the beginnings of Hinduism on the banks of the Indus River. Then move on to the sacred Ganges River and meet Siddhartha Gautama, the founder of Buddhism. Learn how the ruler Asoka expanded and united the Indian empire. Then sit back and enjoy a Jataka Tale.

Lesson Objectives

- Define citadel as a large, round building shaped like a mound.
- Explain that the early people of the Indus Valley built citadel cities.
- Locate the Indus River on a map.

PREPARE

Approximate lesson time is 60 minutes.

Materials

For the Student

    📖 map of the Indian Subcontinent

    globe, inflatable

    pencils, no. 2

    paper, 8 1/2" x 11"

    pencils, colored, 16 or more

    cardboard, sheets

    clay, colored

    leaf

    paper, colored construction, 12"x12" - brown, blue

    twigs - several

    pipe cleaners

    scissors, round-end safety

    📖 I'm Thinking of Something activity sheet

    crayons, 16 or more

Keywords and Pronunciation

citadel (SIH-tuh-dl) : A large, round building shaped like a mound.
Mohenjo-Daro (moh-HEN-joh DAHR-oh)

LEARN
Activity 1: A Look Back *(Online)*

Activity 2: Civilization Along the Indus River *(Online)*

Activity 3: The Mystery of Mohenjo-Daro *(Online)*

Activity 4: History Record Book *(Offline)*

Activity 5. Optional: Citadel City Diorama *(Offline)*

Activity 6. Optional: I'm Thinking of Something *(Offline)*

ASSESS

Lesson Assessment: The Mystery of Mohenjo-Daro (*Offline*)

You will complete an offline assessment covering the main objectives of this lesson. Your learning coach will score this assessment.

LEARN
Activity 7. Optional: More of the Indus Valley Civilization *(Online)*

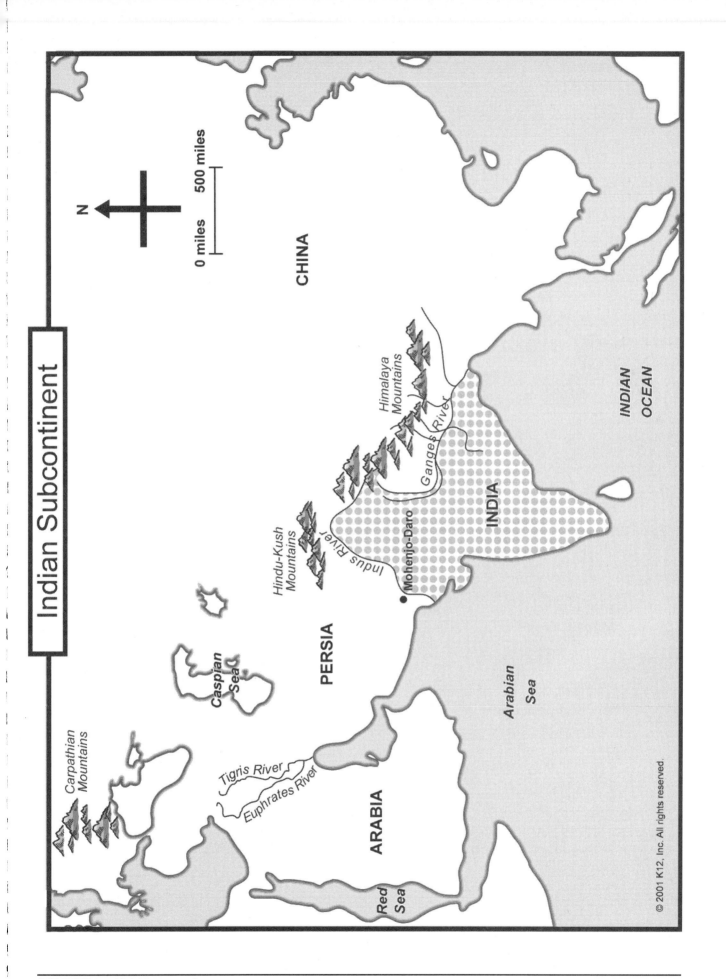

Indian Subcontinent

N

500 miles

0 miles

CHINA

Himalaya Mountains

Ganges River

Hindu-Kush Mountains

Indus River

Mohenjo-Daro

INDIA

INDIAN OCEAN

PERSIA

Caspian Sea

Carpathian Mountains

Tigris River

Euphrates River

ARABIA

Arabian Sea

Red Sea

Name _____   Date _____

I'm Thinking of Something

Listen carefully as a series of items are described. Find each item on the page and color it. After you have found all the items, color the rest of the page.

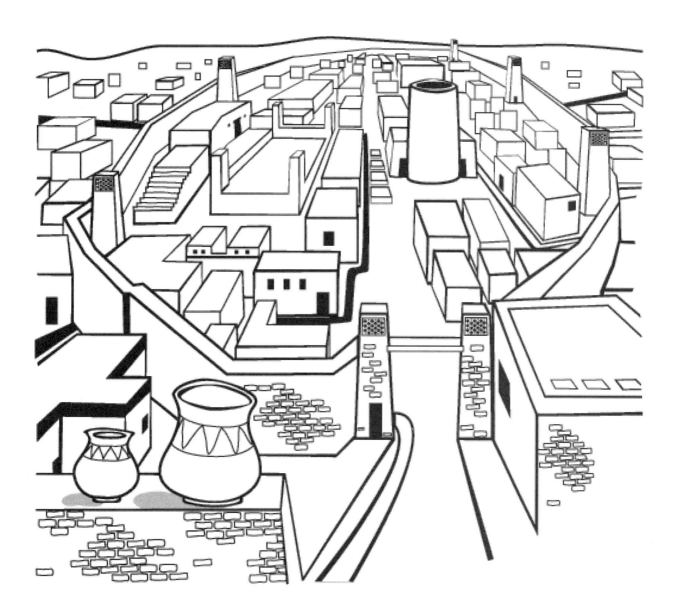

Name _____   Date _____

Lesson Assessment

The Mystery of Mohenjo-Daro

To answer question 1, please use the map of the Indian Subcontinent.

1. Where is the Indus River located?

2. What did the early people of the Indus Valley build?

3. Ancient cities along the Indus River were built around citadels. What were these citadels?

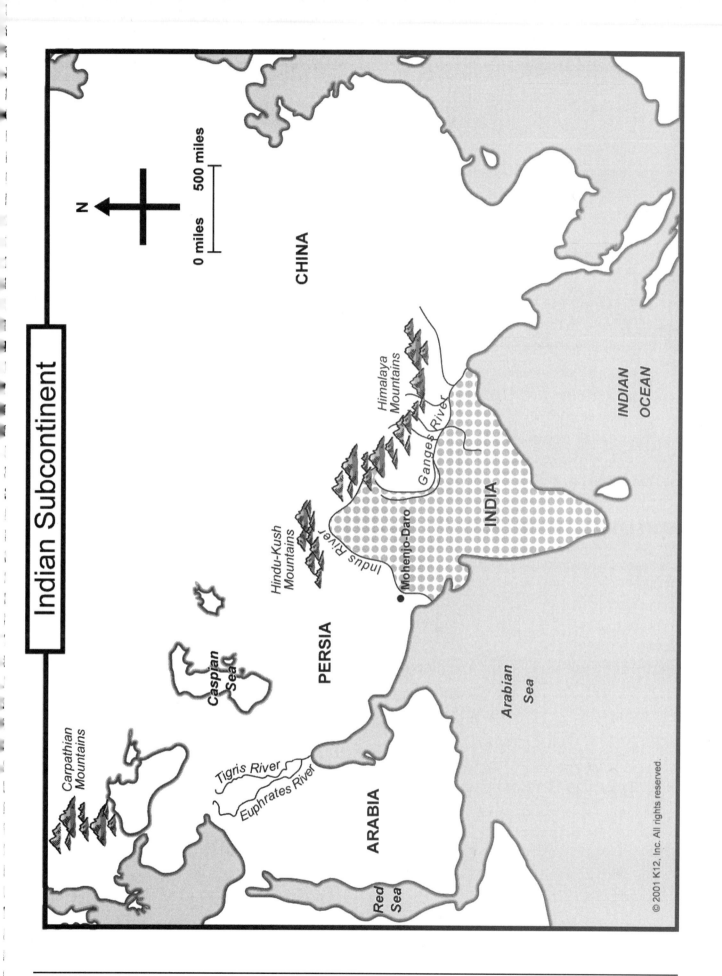

Indian Subcontinent

N

500 miles

0 miles

CHINA

Carpathian
Mountains

Caspian
Sea

Hindu-Kush
Mountains

Himalaya
Mountains

Ganges River

Indus River

Mohenjo-Daro

INDIA

PERSIA

Tigris River

Euphrates River

ARABIA

Red
Sea

Arabian
Sea

INDIAN
OCEAN

Student Guide
Lesson 2: Ancient Hinduism

Lesson Objectives

- Name Hinduism as a very old religion that began near the Indus River.
- Describe the Hindu religion as having many gods and goddesses.
- Explain that there is one great power called Brahman in the Hindu religion.

PREPARE

Approximate lesson time is 60 minutes.

Materials

For the Student

📖 map of the Indian Subcontinent

pencils, no. 2

paper, 8 1/2" x 11"

pencils, colored, 16 or more

📖 Hindu Gods coloring page

crayons, 16 or more

Lights for Gita by Rachna Gilmore

Keywords and Pronunciation

Brahma (BRAH-muh)

Brahmans (BRAH-muhns)

Hinduism (HIN-doo-ih-zuhm)

Hindus (HIN-doos)

Shiva (SHIH-vuh)

Vedas (VAY-duhz)

Vishnu (VISH-noo)

LEARN
Activity 1: A Quick Review *(Online)*

Activity 2: The Rise of Hinduism *(Online)*

Activity 3: Ancient Hinduism *(Online)*

Activity 4: History Record Book *(Offline)*

Activity 5. Optional: Some Hindu Gods *(Offline)*

Activity 6. Optional: Hindu Web *(Offline)*

ASSESS

Lesson Assessment: Ancient Hinduism (*Offline*)

You will complete an offline assessment covering the main objectives of this lesson. Your learning coach will score this assessment.

LEARN
Activity 7. Optional: Krishna *(Offline)*

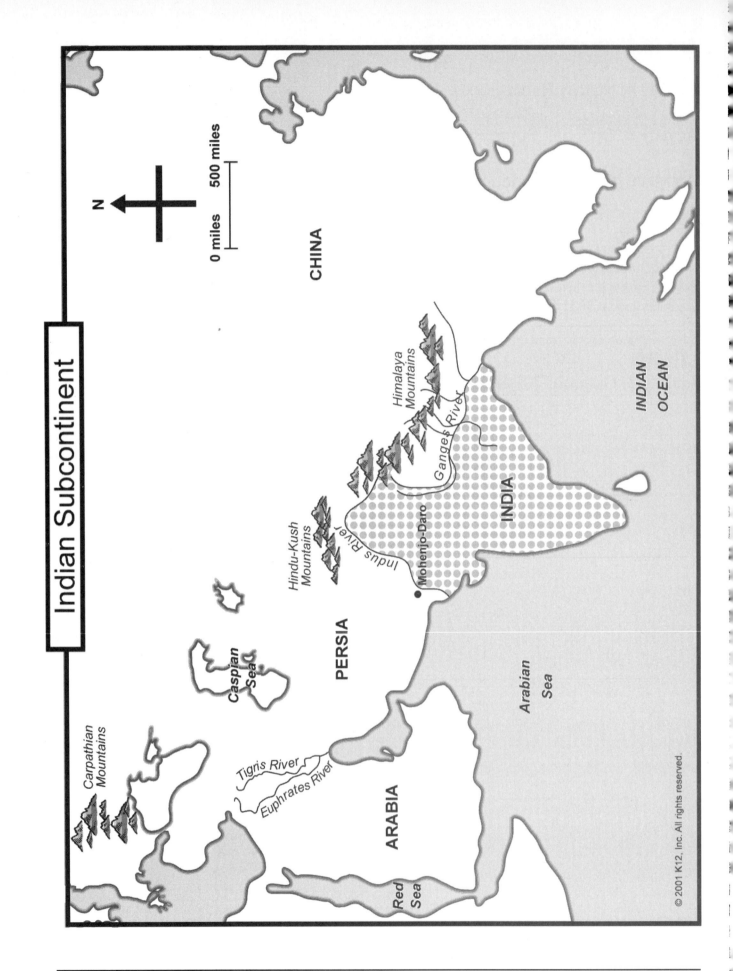

Indian Subcontinent

N

0 miles
500 miles

CHINA

Himalaya Mountains

Ganges River

Hindu-Kush Mountains

Indus River

Mohenjo-Daro

INDIA

PERSIA

INDIAN OCEAN

Caspian Sea

Arabian Sea

Carpathian Mountains

Tigris River

Euphrates River

ARABIA

Red Sea

Name _____   Date _____

Lesson Assessment

Ancient Hinduism

1. What is the name of the very old religion that you learned about today?

2. Where did it begin?

3. Do Hindus believe in one God or many gods and goddesses?

4. Hindus also believe in one great power that is present in all things and rules all things, even the gods and goddesses. What do they call this one great power?

Student Guide
Lesson 3: The Ganges River

Lesson Objectives

- Locate the Indian subcontinent on a map.
- Locate the Ganges River on a map.
- State that the Hindus consider the Ganges River to be sacred.

PREPARE

Approximate lesson time is 60 minutes.

Materials

For the Student

    📖 map of the Indian Subcontinent

    crayons, 16 or more

    pencils, no. 2

    paper, 8 1/2" x 11"

    pencils, colored, 16 or more

    clay, colored - blue, gray, brown, green

    Sacred River by Ted Lewin

Keywords and Pronunciation

Ganga (GAHNG-uh)

Ganges (GAN-jeez)

Himalaya (hih-muh-LAY-uh)

relief map : A map that uses texture to show topographical features such as mountains, hills, and plateaus.

Shiva (SHIH-vuh)

subcontinent : A large piece of land, but not large enough to be a continent; a large piece of land that is part of a continent.

LEARN
Activity 1: A Quick Review *(Online)*

Activity 2: East to the Ganges *(Online)*

Activity 3: Ganga, the River Goddess *(Online)*

Activity 4: The Ganges River *(Online)*

Activity 5: History Record Book *(Offline)*

Activity 6. Optional: Relief Map of the Indian Subcontinent *(Offline)*

Activity 7. Optional: The Sacred Ganges River *(Offline)*

ASSESS

Lesson Assessment: The Ganges River *(Offline)*

You will complete an offline assessment covering the main objectives of this lesson. Your learning coach will score this assessment.

LEARN
Activity 8. Optional: Read Aloud *(Offline)*

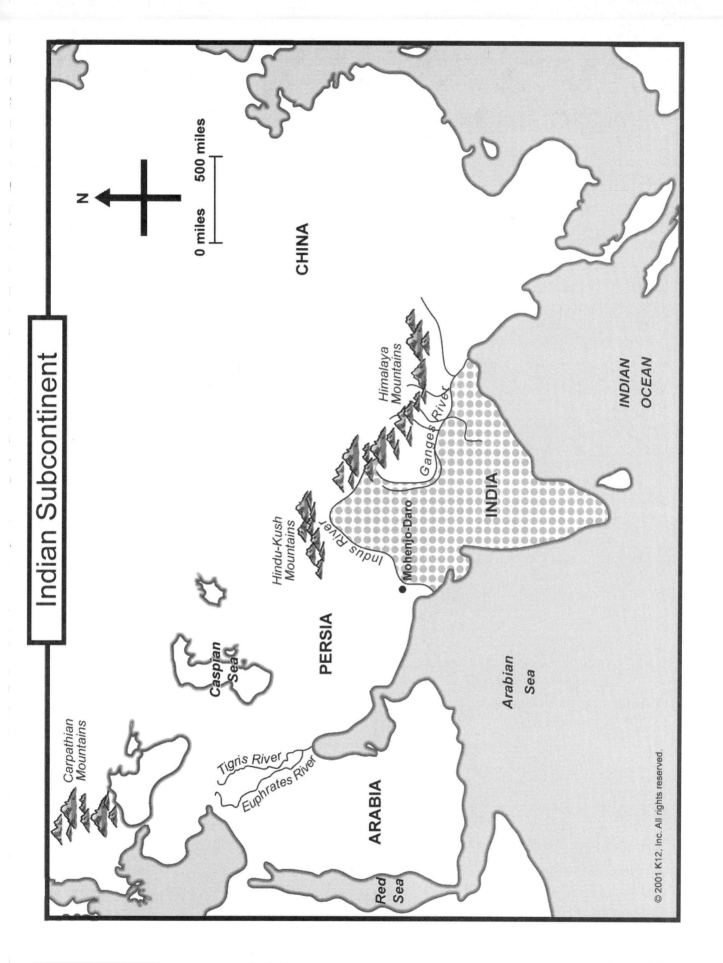

Indian Subcontinent

CHINA

500 miles

0 miles

N

Himalaya Mountains

Ganges River

INDIA

INDIAN OCEAN

Hindu-Kush Mountains

Indus River

Mohenjo-Daro

PERSIA

Caspian Sea

Carpathian Mountains

Tigris River

Euphrates River

ARABIA

Arabian Sea

Red Sea

© 2001 K12, Inc. All rights reserved.

Lesson Assessment

The Ganges River

To answer this question, please use the map of the world.

1. Where is the Indian subcontinent located?

To answer this question, please use the map of the Indian Subcontinent.

2. Where is the Ganges River located?

3. Which religion considers the Ganges River a sacred river?

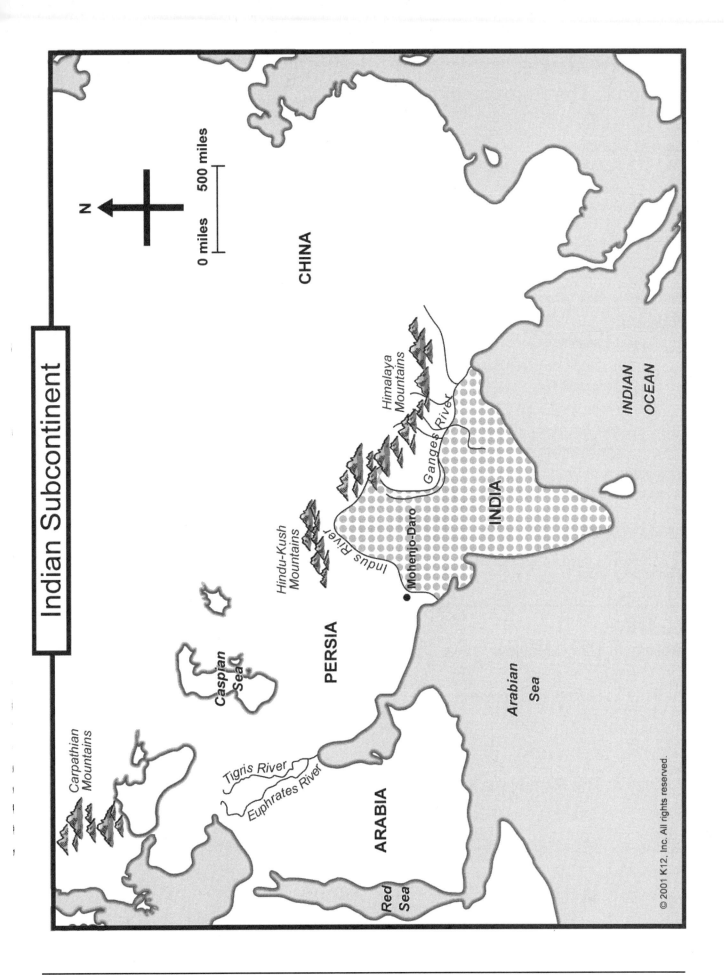

Indian Subcontinent

N

500 miles

0 miles

CHINA

Himalaya Mountains

Ganges River

Hindu-Kush Mountains

Indus River

INDIA

Mohenjo-Daro

INDIAN OCEAN

Caspian Sea

PERSIA

Carpathian Mountains

Arabian Sea

Tigris River

Euphrates River

ARABIA

Red Sea

Student Guide
Lesson 4: The Ramayana

Lesson Objectives

- Explain that in a story from the Ramayana, the god Vishnu became a prince named Rama and defeated an evil king.
- Identify the Ramayana as a sacred Hindu book.

PREPARE

Approximate lesson time is 60 minutes.

Materials

For the Student

- map of the Indian Subcontinent
- pencils, no. 2
- paper, 8 1/2" x 11"
- pencils, colored, 16 or more
- crayons, 16 or more

Keywords and Pronunciation

Rama (RAH-muh)
Ramayana (rah-muh-YAH-nuh)
Ravana (RAH-vuh-nh)
Sita (SEE-tuh)
Vishnu (VISH-noo)

LEARN
Activity 1: Hindu Review *(Online)*

Activity 2: Rama and Ravana *(Online)*

Activity 3: The Ramayana *(Online)*

Activity 4: History Record Book *(Offline)*

Activity 5. Optional: Coloring Pages *(Offline)*

Activity 6. Optional: Sacred Book *(Offline)*

ASSESS

Lesson Assessment: The Ramayana (*Offline*)

You will complete an offline assessment covering the main objectives of this lesson. Your learning coach will score this assessment.

LEARN

Activity 7. Optional: Library Search *(Offline)*

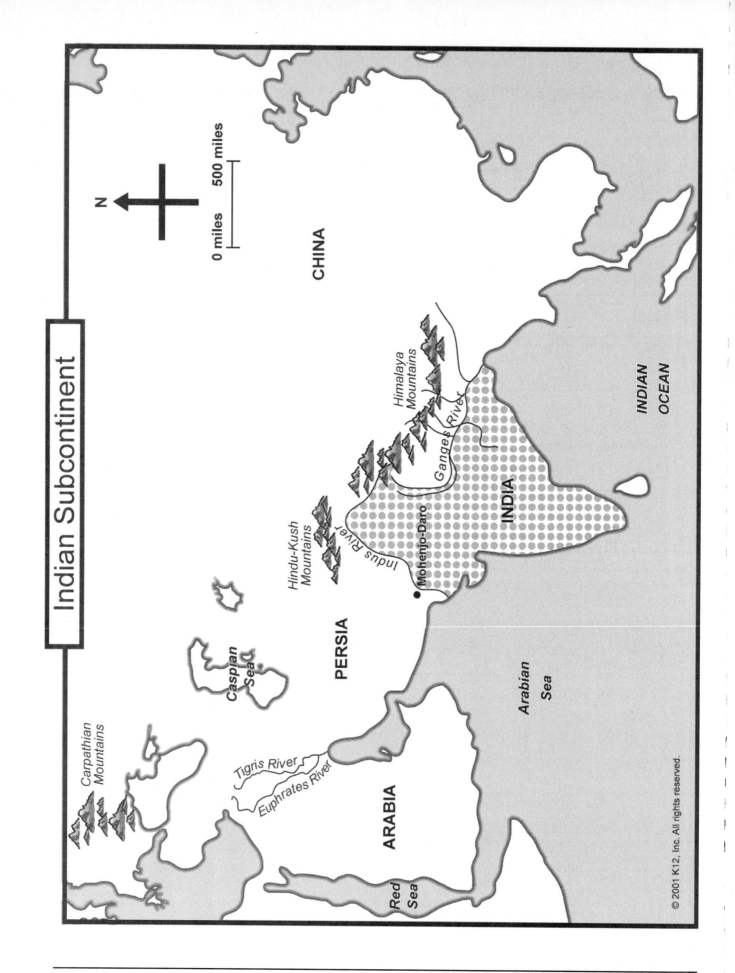

Indian Subcontinent

N

500 miles

0 miles

CHINA

Himalaya Mountains

Ganges River

Hindu-Kush Mountains

INDIA

Indus River

Mohenjo-Daro

INDIAN OCEAN

Caspian Sea

PERSIA

Carpathian Mountains

Arabian Sea

Tigris River

Euphrates River

ARABIA

Red Sea

Name _____ Date _____

Lesson Assessment

The Ramayana

1. What is the Ramayana?

2. In the story we read, the god Vishnu came down to Earth and became a prince. What was the prince's name?

3. Who helped Rama fight the evil king?

Student Guide
Lesson 5: Siddhartha Gautama: The Buddha

Lesson Objectives

- Summarize the story of how Siddhartha became the Buddha.
- Identify Siddhartha Gautama as the Buddha, the person who started Buddhism.
- Explain that Siddhartha Gautama was an Indian prince.

PREPARE

Approximate lesson time is 60 minutes.

Materials

For the Student

    🖳 map of the Indian Subcontinent

    globe, inflatable

    pencils, no. 2

    paper, 8 1/2" x 11"

    pencils, colored, 16 or more

    🖳 Siddhartha Thinks activity sheet

    crayons, 16 or more

    paper, drawing, 12" x 18"

Keywords and Pronunciation

Buddha (BOO-duh)

Buddhism (BOO-dih-zuhm)

Buddhists (BOO-dists)

Himalaya (hih-muh-LAY-uh)

Siddhartha Gautama (*sid-DAHR-tuh GOW-tuh-muh*)

LEARN
Activity 1: Locating India *(Online)*

Activity 2: Siddhartha, the Young Prince *(Online)*

Activity 3: Siddhartha Gautama: The Buddha *(Online)*

Activity 4: History Record Book *(Offline)*

Activity 5. Optional: Siddhartha Thinks *(Offline)*

Activity 6. Optional: Think About It *(Offline)*

ASSESS

Lesson Assessment: Siddhartha Gautama: The Buddha (*Offline*)

You will complete an offline assessment covering the main objectives of this lesson. Your learning coach will score this assessment.

LEARN

Activity 7. Optional: More Thinking *(Offline)*

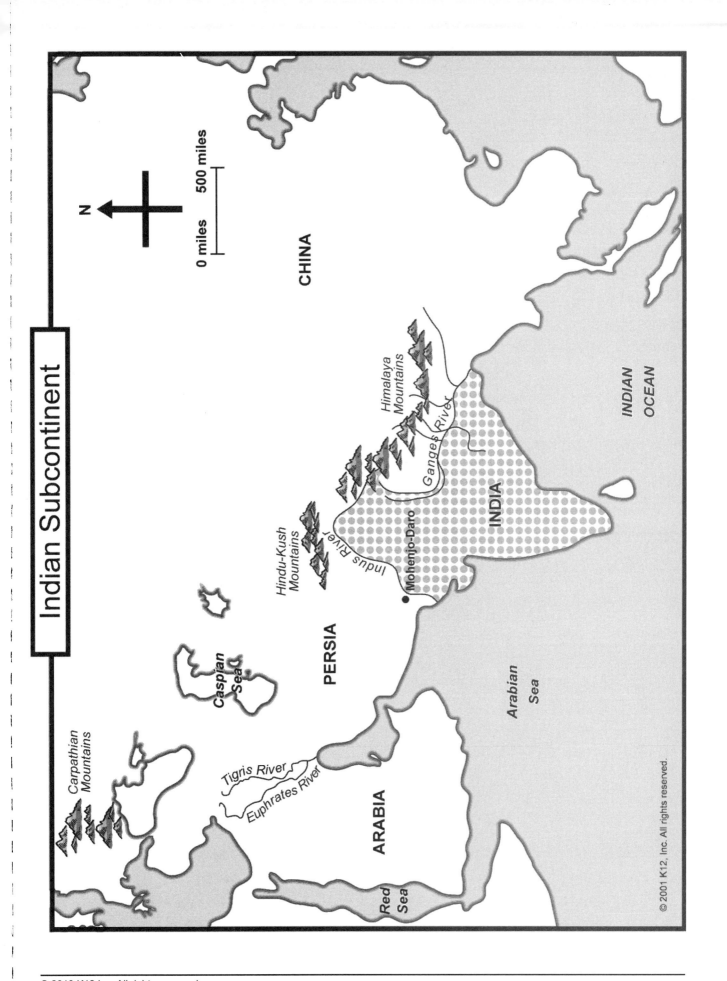

Indian Subcontinent

500 miles

0 miles

N

CHINA

Himalaya Mountains

Ganges River

Hindu-Kush Mountains

Indus River

Mohenjo-Daro

INDIA

INDIAN OCEAN

PERSIA

Caspian Sea

Carpathian Mountains

Tigris River

Euphrates River

ARABIA

Arabian Sea

Red Sea

Name _____   Date _____

Siddhartha Thinks

Think about the story of *Siddhartha, The Young Prince*. Read the words inside the leaves. Color all the leaves that tell about the people dark green. Color all the words that tell about the places light green. Color all the words that tell about Siddhartha's feelings yellow. Color the rest of the picture using the colors you think are best.

Lesson Assessment

Siddhartha Gautama: The Buddha

1. Was Siddhartha Gautama a king or a prince?

2. Siddhartha Gautama became known by a new name. What was it?

3. What do we call the religion that is based on the Buddha's teachings?

4. Summarize the story of *Siddhartha, The Young Prince.*

Student Guide
Lesson 6: Asoka and the Spread of Buddhism

Lesson Objectives

- Identify Asoka as a famous ruler of India.
- Explain that Asoka expanded the empire of India and helped unite it.
- Explain that Asoka converted to Buddhism and tried to spread this religion.

PREPARE

Approximate lesson time is 60 minutes.

Materials

For the Student

    🖳 map of the Indian Subcontinent

    crayons, 16 or more

    pencils, no. 2

    paper, drawing, 12" x 18"

    🖳 King Asoka's Pillar activity sheet

    glue sticks

    scissors, round-end safety

Keywords and Pronunciation

Asoka (uh-SOH-kuh)

stupa (STOO-puh)

LEARN
Activity 1: Looking Back at Buddhism *(Online)*

Activity 2: Asoka's Empire *(Online)*

Activity 3: Asoka: The King Who Changed *(Online)*

Activity 4: The Rest of Asoka's Life *(Online)*

Activity 5: Asoka and the Spread of Buddhism *(Online)*

Activity 6: History Record Book *(Offline)*

Activity 7. Optional: Asoka Has a Change of Heart *(Offline)*

Activity 8. Optional: Asoka's Pillar *(Offline)*

ASSESS

Lesson Assessment: Asoka and the Spread of Buddhism (*Offline*)

You will complete an offline assessment covering the main objectives of this lesson. Your learning coach will score this assessment.

LEARN

Activity 9. Optional: More About Asoka *(Offline)*

Indian Subcontinent

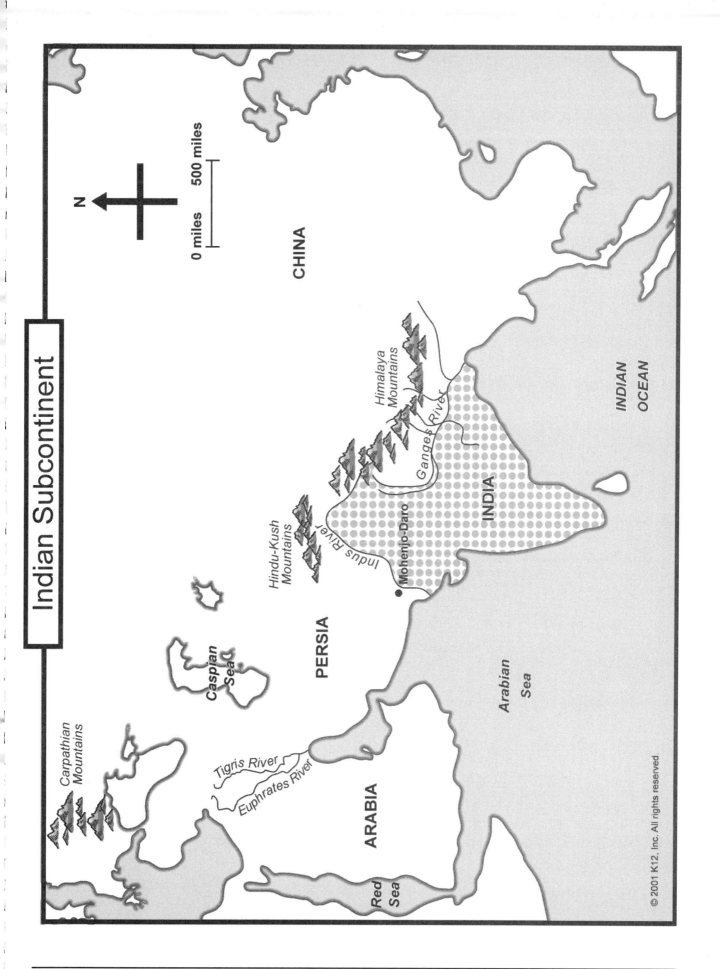

Name   Date

King Asoka's Pillar

Read the words in the boxes. Decide which three of the boxes tell how King Asoka wanted others to behave. Cut these out and glue them in the spaces under the lions' chins. The fourth lion is hiding. Write a sentence on the back of this paper to show something else King Asoka would have wanted.

cut

Be kind to each other.   Have a war.   Say mean words.   Give medicine to the sick.   Fight with your brother.   Help animals.

Lesson Assessment

Asoka and the Spread of Buddhism

1. What was the name of the ruler we learned about today?

2. What empire did Asoka rule?

3. At first, how did Asoka expand his empire?

4. After a while Asoka decided to give up making war and unite his people by winning their hearts. What religion did he decide to follow?

Student Guide
Lesson 7: A Jataka Tale: The Monkey King

Lesson Objectives

- Demonstrate mastery of important knowledge and skills in this unit.
- Identify the Jataka Tales as stories that illustrate Buddhist teachings about how to live a good life.
- Explain that the early people of the Indus Valley built citadel cities.
- Locate the Indus River on a map.
- Describe the Hindu religion as having many gods and goddesses.
- Locate the Ganges River on a map.
- State that the Hindus consider the Ganges River to be sacred.
- Identify the Ramayana as a sacred Hindu book.
- Identify Siddhartha Gautama as the Buddha, the person who started Buddhism.
- Explain that Asoka converted to Buddhism and tried to spread this religion.

PREPARE

Approximate lesson time is 60 minutes.

Materials

For the Student

- map of the Indian Subcontinent
- Monkey King Puppets activity sheet

crayons, 16 or more

pencils, no. 2

Elmer's Glue-All

markers, colored, 8 or more

paper, drawing, 12" x 18"

popsicle sticks

scissors, round-end safety

tape, clear

pencils, colored, 16 or more

Keywords and Pronunciation

Jataka (JAH-tuh-kuh)

LEARN
Activity 1: A Quick Review *(Online)*

Activity 2: The Monkey King *(Online)*

Activity 3. Optional: Monkey King Puppets *(Offline)*

Activity 4: Reviewing Unit Seven *(Online)*

ASSESS
Unit Assessment: Ancient India *(Offline)*

Complete an offline Unit Assessment. Your learning coach will score this part of the Assessment.

LEARN
Activity 5. Optional: Your Own Jataka Tale *(Offline)*

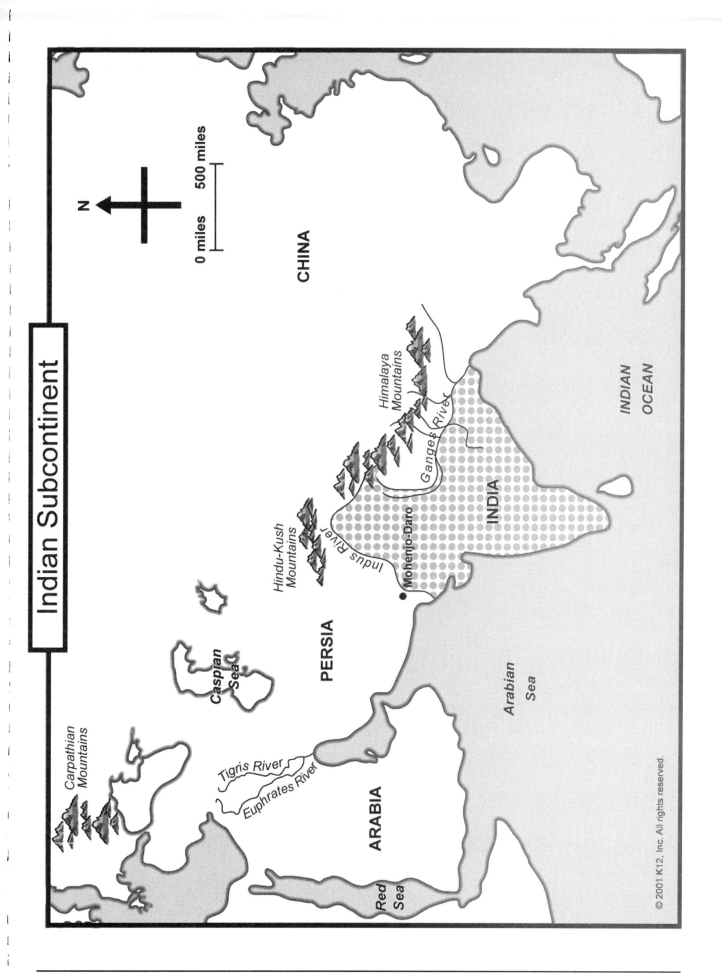

Indian Subcontinent

CHINA

500 miles

0 miles

N

Himalaya Mountains

Ganges River

INDIA

INDIAN OCEAN

Hindu-Kush Mountains

Indus River

Mohenjo-Daro

PERSIA

Caspian Sea

Carpathian Mountains

Arabian Sea

Tigris River

Euphrates River

ARABIA

Red Sea

© 2001 K12, Inc. All rights reserved.

Monkey King Puppets

Color the pictures. Then cut each one out and glue or tape it to a Popsicle stick. Draw a river, mango tree, and some other trees on a piece of drawing paper for background. Then use your Monkey King Puppets to act out the story.

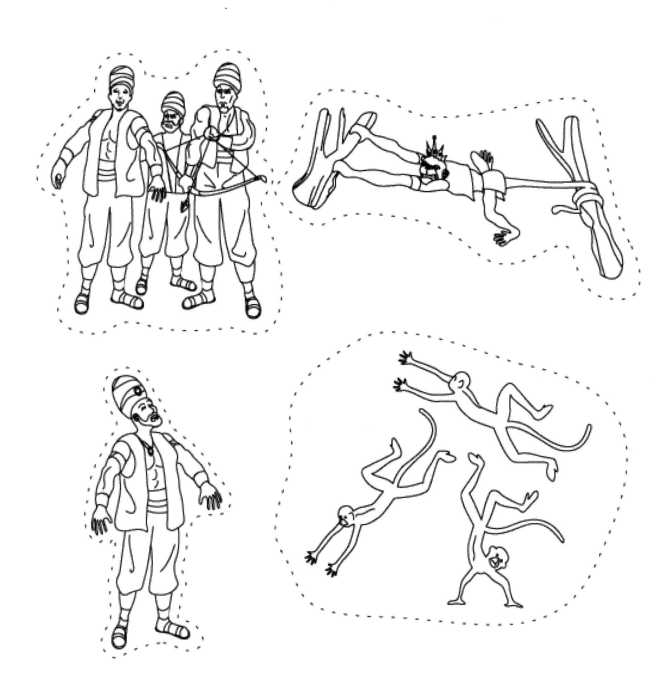

<u>Name</u>   Date

Ancient India

Select the one best answer. Shade or color the bubble for the answer you choose.

1. Which is the Indian religion that has many gods and goddesses?
   - ○ Vishnuism
   - ○ Hinduism
   - ○ Judaism

2. What is the main reason that people settled down and built cities near the Indus River?
   - ○ because the river let them enjoy water sports
   - ○ because the river provided water to drink and to grow crops
   - ○ because the river protected them against attackers

3. What are Brahma, Vishnu, and Shiva?
   - ○ three main gods of Hinduism
   - ○ three rivers in India
   - ○ three cities in the Indus River valley

4. What river is sacred to Hindus?
   - ○ Ganges
   - ○ Tigris
   - ○ Nile

5. Which of these is a sacred Hindu book?
   - ○ the Jataka
   - ○ the Ramayana
   - ○ the Gautama

6. Who is known as the *Buddha* — the founder of Buddhism?
   - ○ Prince Rama
   - ○ Vishnu the Preserver
   - ○ Siddartha Gautama

7. What did Asoka do?
   - ○ write the Jataka Tales
   - ○ help spread Buddhism beyond India
   - ○ defeat an evil king

8. The map below shows two main rivers of ancient India. What are the names of these rivers?
   - ○ Tigris and Euphrates
   - ○ Nile and Niger
   - ○ Indus and Ganges

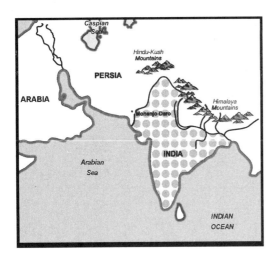

Student Guide
Lesson 1: Farming in Ancient China

Making silk and writing calligraphy were two of the arts begun in ancient China, where the Yellow and Yangtze Rivers flowed. Learn about the important teacher Confucius and the famous Great Wall. See the life-size soldiers guarding the tomb of Emperor Qin Shi Huangdi. Then enter the inventive times of the Han Dynasty.

Lesson Objectives

- Locate China on a map.
- Locate the Yellow and Yangtze Rivers.
- Explain that the annual flooding of rivers allowed people to grow grain such as rice.

PREPARE

Approximate lesson time is 60 minutes.

Materials

For the Student

    📖 map of Ancient China

    History Record Book

    rice

    crayons, 16 or more

    pencils, no. 2

    paper, 8 1/2" x 11"

    📖 Planting Rice Along the River activity sheet

    Growing Up in Ancient China by Ken Teague

    Li Lun: Lad of Courage by Carolyn Treffinger (ISBN 0-8027-7468-7)

Keywords and Pronunciation

Yangtze (YANG-see)

LEARN
Activity 1: Reviewing Rivers *(Online)*

Activity 2: Life Along the Yellow River *(Online)*

Activity 3: Life Along the Yangtze River *(Online)*

Activity 4: Lu Listens to the River *(Online)*

Activity 5: Farming in Ancient China *(Online)*

Activity 6: History Record Book *(Offline)*

Activity 7. Optional: Lu Explores the Rivers *(Online)*

Activity 8. Optional: Planting Rice Along the River *(Offline)*

ASSESS

Lesson Assessment: Farming in Ancient China (*Offline*)

You will complete an offline assessment covering the main objectives of this lesson. Your learning coach will score this assessment.

LEARN

Activity 9. Optional: Read On *(Offline)*

Ancient China

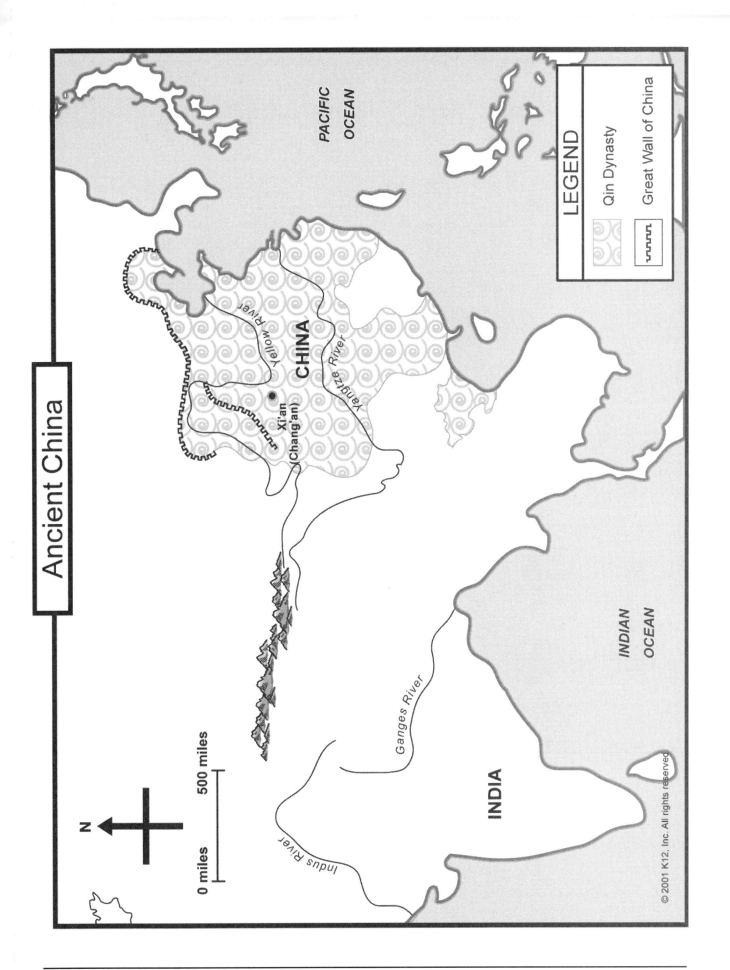

PACIFIC OCEAN

CHINA

Yellow River

Yangtze River

Xi'an (Chang'an)

INDIA

Ganges River

Indus River

INDIAN OCEAN

N

0 miles

500 miles

LEGEND

Qin Dynasty

Great Wall of China

Name _____   Date _____

Planting Rice Along the River

Read the sentences. Decide which ones tell something that would happen or be done so that rice would grow for Lu and his family. Cross out the sentences that don't belong. Then color the picture.

1. Flooding river waters fill the rice paddies.

2. The rice paddies freeze.

3. The Yangtze waters drain back into the river.

4. The rice paddies become completely dry.

5. Farmers plow the fields and plant rice in straight rows.

6. The long stalks grow until they are heavy with rice.

7. The rice drops off the stalks and the farmers pick it up.

8. Farmers cut the rice stalks with sickles.

Lesson Assessment

Farming in Ancient China

1. To answer this question, please use the map of the world. Where is China located?

2. To answer this question, please use the map of Ancient China. Where is the Yellow River located?

3. To answer this question, please use the map of Ancient China. Where is the Yangtze River located?

4. How did the rivers help people grow food?

5. What did the Chinese people do with the discovery of silk?

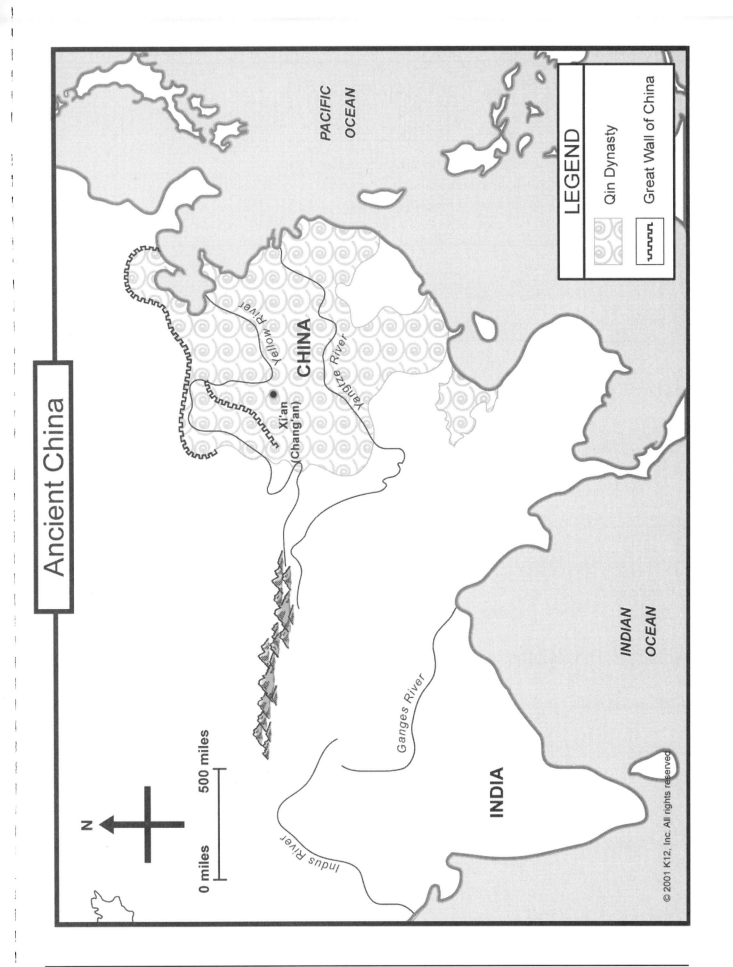

Ancient China

PACIFIC OCEAN

LEGEND
Qin Dynasty
Great Wall of China

CHINA

Yellow River

Yangtze River

Xi'an (Chang'an)

INDIA

Ganges River

Indus River

INDIAN OCEAN

N

500 miles

0 miles

© 2001 K12, Inc. All rights reserved.

Student Guide
Lesson 2: Early China: The Discovery of Silk

Lesson Objectives

- Explain that China became famous for silk cloth produced there.
- Explain that silk comes from silkworms.
- Explain that the ancient Chinese discovered how to make silk.

PREPARE

Approximate lesson time is 60 minutes.

Materials

For the Student

  🖳 map of Ancient China

  pencils, no. 2

  paper, 8 1/2" x 11"

  pencils, colored, 16 or more

  🖳 Making Silk coloring page

  crayons, 16 or more

  clothing - silk and other fabrics

Keywords and Pronunciation

Min Lai (min liy)

LEARN
Activity 1: A Quick Review *(Online)*

Activity 2: The Empress's Great Discovery *(Online)*

Activity 3: Making Silk *(Online)*

Activity 4: Early China: The Discovery of Silk *(Online)*

Activity 5: History Record Book *(Offline)*

Activity 6. Optional: The Art of Making Silk *(Offline)*

Activity 7. Optional: Discovering Silk *(Offline)*

ASSESS

Lesson Assessment: Early China: The Discovery of Silk *(Offline)*

You will complete an offline assessment covering the main objectives of this lesson. Your learning coach will score this assessment.

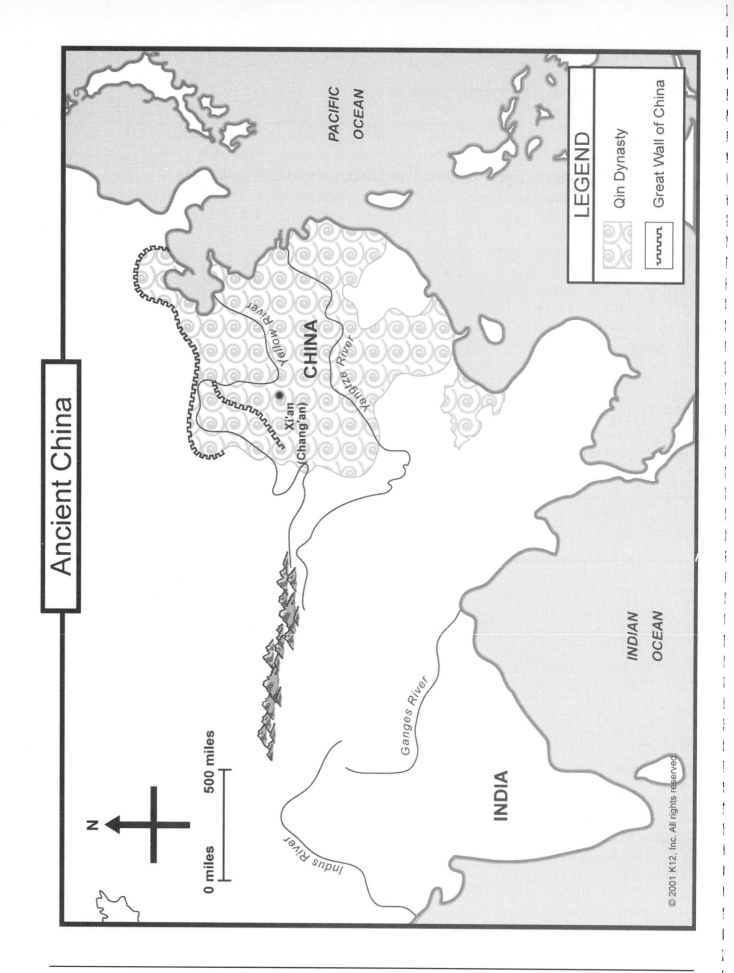

Ancient China

PACIFIC OCEAN

LEGEND

Qin Dynasty

Great Wall of China

CHINA

Yellow River

Yangtze River

Xi'an (Chang'an)

Ganges River

Indus River

INDIA

INDIAN OCEAN

N

0 miles

500 miles

1. Women collected and sorted the cocoons.

2. Women boiled each cocoon and carefully pulled out the single strand of silk

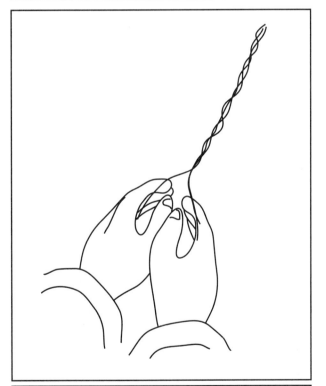

3. The strands were twisted together into threads.

4. The threads were dyed and woven into cloth.

Lesson Assessment

Early China: The Discovery of Silk

1. We read a story about an empress who made a great discovery long ago. What land did she live in?

2. According to the legend, what fell into the empress's cup of tea?

3. What kind of thread did she make from the cocoon?

4. What did the Chinese people do with the discovery of silk?

Student Guide
Lesson 3: Chinese Calligraphy

Lesson Objectives

- Define calligraphy as artistic handwriting.
- Explain that ancient Chinese wrote by drawing pictures that stood for words.

PREPARE

Approximate lesson time is 60 minutes.

Materials

For the Student

- map of Ancient China
- Characters Galore activity sheet

  markers, colored, 8 or more

  crayons, 16 or more

  paper, 8 1/2" x 11"

  pencils, colored, 16 or more

- Be a Calligrapher

  paintbrush

  paints, watercolor, 8 colors or more

  paper, drawing, 12" x 18"

  Long Is a Dragon: Chinese Writing for Children by Peggy Goldstein

Keywords and Pronunciation
calligrapher (kuh-LIH-gruh-fuhr)
calligraphy (kuh-LIH-gruh-fee) : An artistic form of handwriting.

LEARN
Activity 1: Questions and Answers *(Online)*

Activity 2: Characters Galore *(Online)*

Activity 3: Chinese Calligraphy *(Online)*

Activity 4: Chinese Calligraphy *(Online)*

Activity 5: History Record Book *(Offline)*

Activity 6. Optional: Be a Calligrapher *(Offline)*

Activity 7. Optional: Drawing On! *(Offline)*

ASSESS

Lesson Assessment: Chinese Calligraphy (*Offline*)

You will complete an offline assessment covering the main objectives of this lesson. Your learning coach will score this assessment.

LEARN
Activity 8. Optional: Chinese Writing *(Offline)*

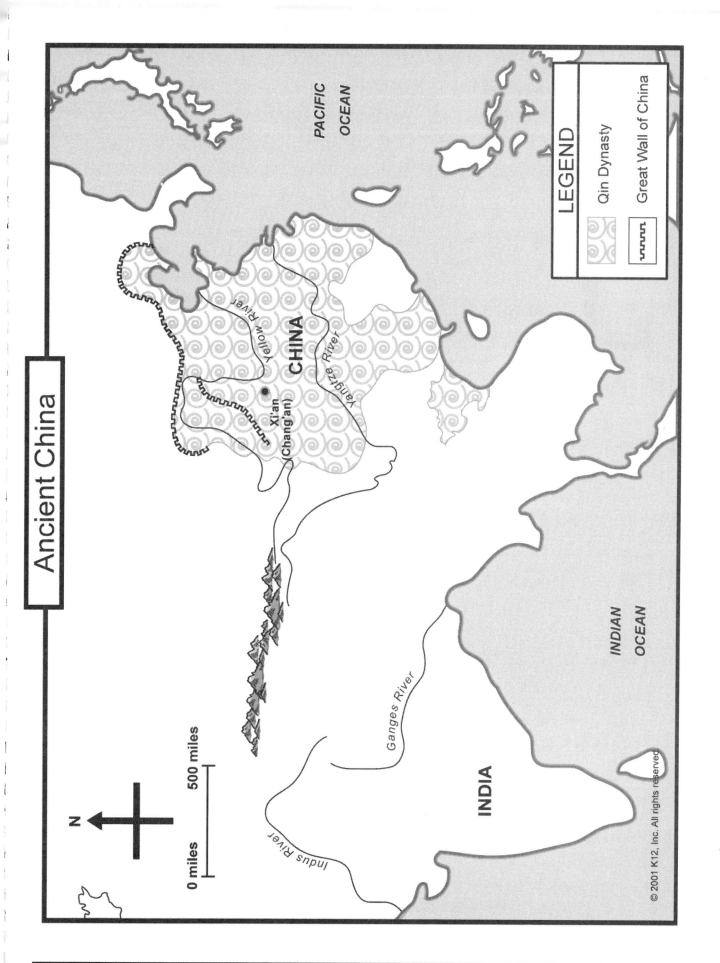

Ancient China

CHINA

INDIA

Yellow River

Yangtze River

Xi'an
(Chang'an)

Ganges River

Indus River

PACIFIC
OCEAN

INDIAN
OCEAN

LEGEND

Qin Dynasty

Great Wall of China

N

0 miles

500 miles

© 2001 K12, Inc. All rights reserved

245

Name _____   Date _____

Characters Galore

Practice drawing the Chinese characters for mountain, fire, and tree.

mountain	fire	tree
山	火	木

Name _____   Date _____

Be A Calligrapher

Here are the Chinese characters for the words sun, water, stars, air, and earth. Use a brush and watercolors to practice making them. Remember that you practiced mountain, fire, tree, and forest as you learned about calligraphy. Now you can make a beautiful world of calligraphy.

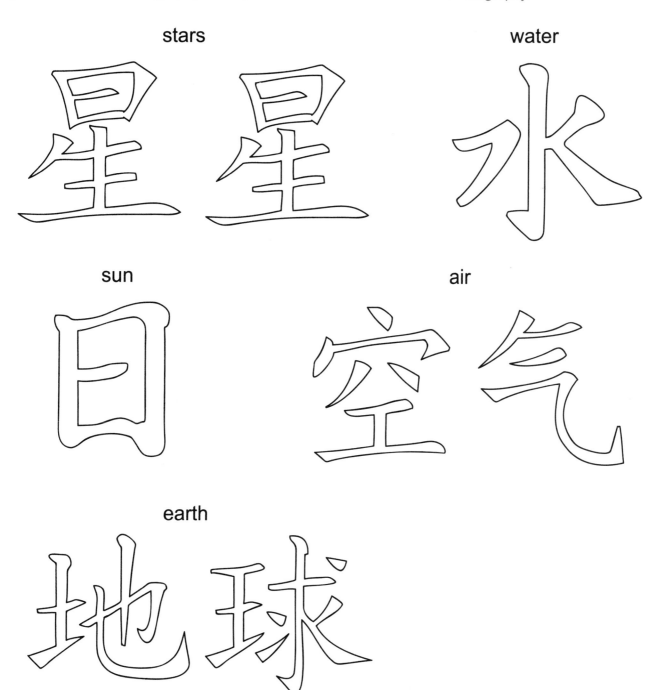

stars

water

sun

air

earth

247

Name _____   Date _____

Lesson Assessment

Chinese Calligraphy

1. Ancient Chinese writers did not use letters like A, B, or C to write. What did they do instead?

2. What is calligraphy?

3. What is a calligrapher?

Student Guide
Lesson 4: Confucius: The Wise Teacher

Lesson Objectives

- Identify Confucius as a teacher in ancient China.
- Explain that Confucius had many sayings to help people live better lives.

PREPARE

Approximate lesson time is 60 minutes.

Materials

For the Student

📖 map of Ancient China

crayons, 16 or more

pencils, no. 2

paper, 8 1/2" x 11"

glue sticks

paper, colored construction, 12"x12"

pencils, colored, 16 or more

scissors, round-end safety

📖 A Rule to Live By activity sheet

Keywords and Pronunciation

Confucius (kuhn-FYOO-shuhs)

LEARN
Activity 1: Rivers, Silk, and Word-Pictures (Online)

Activity 2: The Wise Teacher (Online)

Activity 3: Some of Confucius' Sayings (Online)

Activity 4: Confucius: The Wise Teacher (Online)

Activity 5: History Record Book *(Offline)*

Activity 6. Optional: Confucius Taught Respect *(Offline)*

Activity 7. Optional: A Rule to Live By *(Offline)*

ASSESS

Lesson Assessment: Confucius: The Wise Teacher (*Offline*)

You will complete an offline assessment covering the main objectives of this lesson. Your learning coach will score this assessment.

LEARN

Activity 8. Optional: A Wise Teacher *(Offline)*

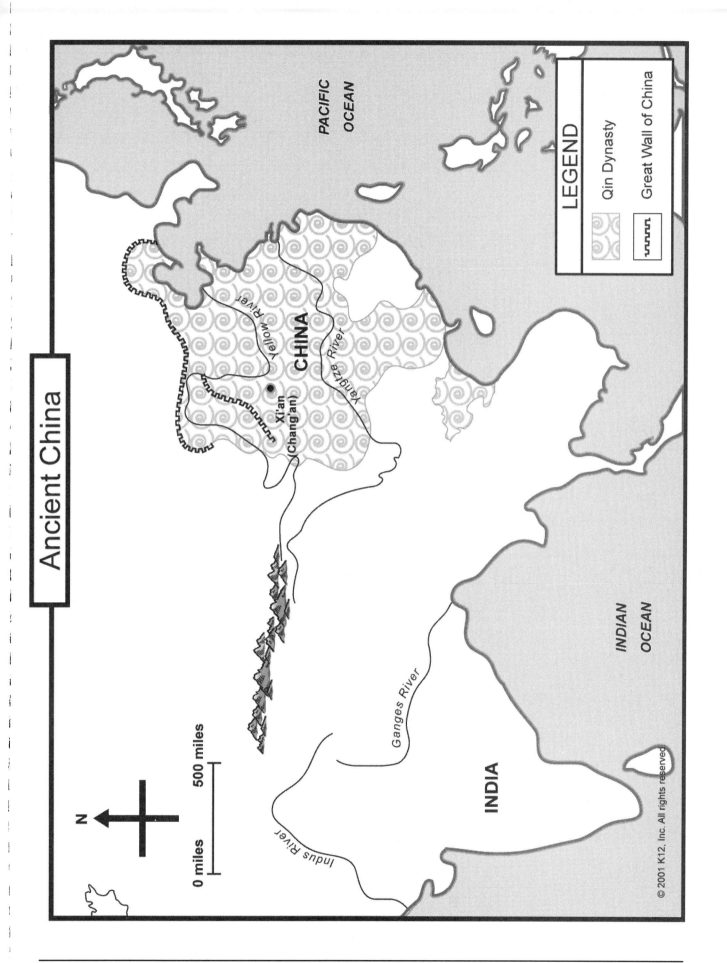

Ancient China

LEGEND
Qin Dynasty
Great Wall of China

PACIFIC OCEAN

CHINA

Yellow River

Yangtze River

Xi'an (Chang'an)

INDIA

Ganges River

Indus River

INDIAN OCEAN

N

0 miles
500 miles

© 2001 K12, Inc. All rights reserved

Name

Date

Confucius said:

Name _____   Date _____

Lesson Assessment

Confucius: The Wise Teacher

1. We learned about a great teacher in ancient China. What is his name?

2. How did people in China remember the things Confucius taught?

3. What did the sayings of Confucius teach people?

Student Guide
Lesson 5: The Emperor Builds a Wall

Lesson Objectives

- Identify Qin Shi Huangdi as the ruler who unified China.
- Explain that the Great Wall was built to keep invaders out of China.

PREPARE

Approximate lesson time is 60 minutes.

Materials

For the Student

    🖥 map of Ancient China

    crayons, 16 or more

    pencils, no. 2

    paper, 8 1/2" x 11"

    cardboard, sheets

    clay, colored

    blocks

    dominoes

    Play-Doh

    scissors, round-end safety

    🖥 Unified China activity sheet

    file folder

    Elmer's Glue-All

    pencils, colored, 16 or more

Keywords and Pronunciation

Qin (chin)

Qin Shi Huangdi (chin shur hwahng-dee)

Zheng (djoong)

LEARN
Activity 1: Let's Review *(Online)*

…

Activity 2: Qin Shi Huangdi *(Online)*

Activity 3: The Emperor Builds a Wall *(Online)*

Activity 4: History Record Book *(Offline)*

Activity 5. Optional: Great Wall of China Model *(Offline)*

Activity 6. Optional: A Unified China *(Offline)*

ASSESS

Lesson Assessment: The Emperor Builds a Wall (*Offline*)

You will complete an offline assessment covering the main objectives of this lesson. Your learning coach will score this assessment.

LEARN

Activity 7. Optional: A Virtual Tour of the Great Wall *(Online)*

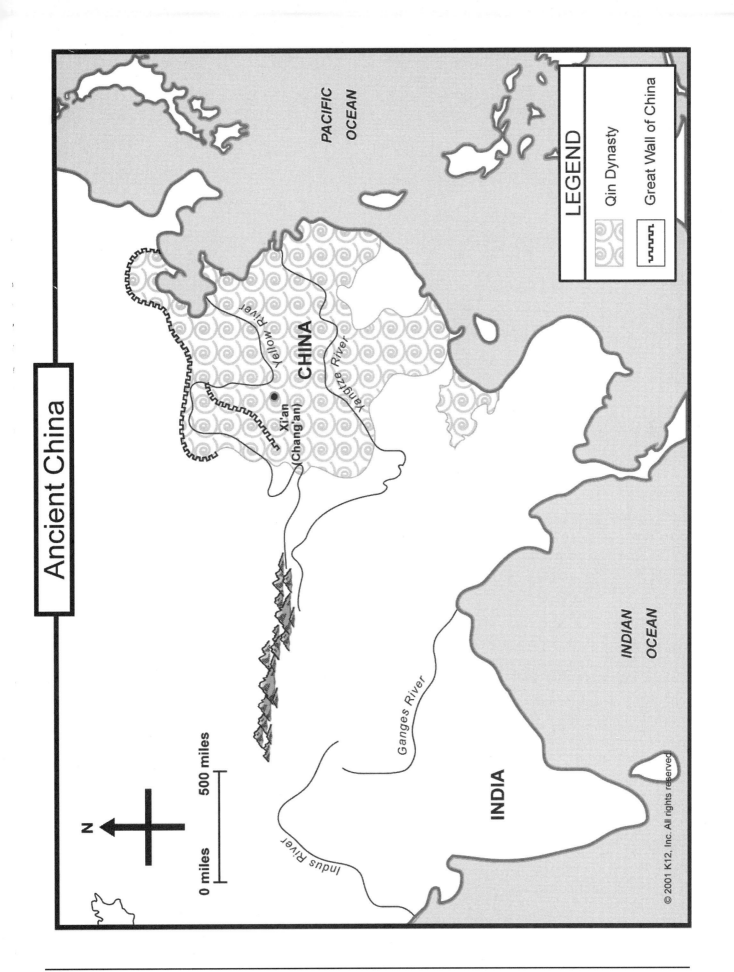

Ancient China

PACIFIC
OCEAN

LEGEND

Qin Dynasty

Great Wall of China

CHINA

Yellow River

Yangtze River

Xi'an
(Chang'an)

INDIA

Ganges River

Indus River

INDIAN
OCEAN

N

500 miles

0 miles

A Unified China

Glue this activity sheet to a manila folder. Cut along the cut lines to make puzzle pieces. Now put the pieces together to make a unified China, just as Qin Shi Huangdi unified many kingdoms into one large empire.

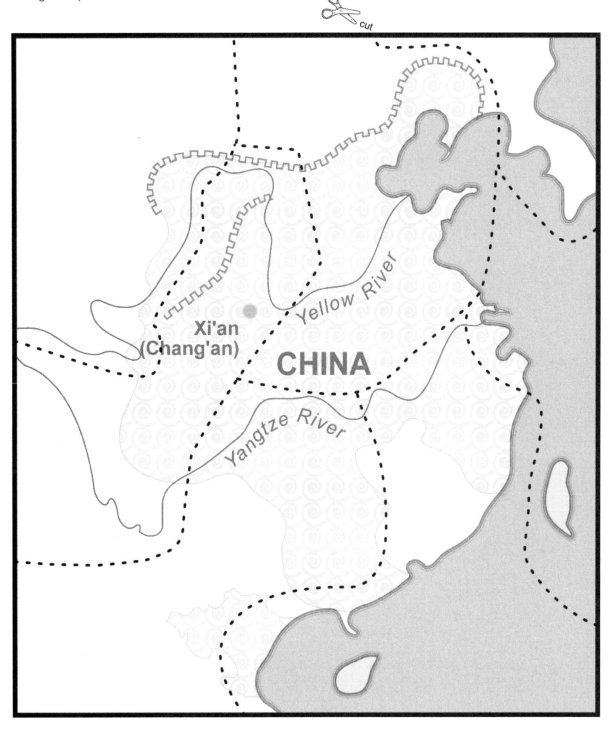

Lesson Assessment

The Emperor Builds a Wall

1. What is the name of the powerful ruler who unified China?

2. Why did Qin Shi Huangdi want to build a Great Wall?

Student Guide
Lesson 6: The Tomb of Qin Shi Huangdi

Lesson Objectives

- Explain that Qin Shi Huangdi built a large underground tomb.
- Describe Qin Shi Huangdi's underground tomb as being full of life-size clay soldiers and horses.

PREPARE

Approximate lesson time is 60 minutes.

Materials

For the Student

📖 map of Ancient China

globe, inflatable

crayons, 16 or more

pencils, no. 2

paper, 8 1/2" x 11"

clay, colored

toothpicks

Keywords and Pronunciation

Xi´an (shee-ahn)

LEARN
Activity 1: Great Wall Review *(Online)*

Activity 2: Qin Shi Huangdi *(Online)*

Activity 3: The Tomb of Qin Shi Huangdi *(Online)*

Activity 4: History Record Book *(Offline)*

Activity 5. Optional: Guarding the Tomb *(Offline)*

Activity 6. Optional: Qin Shi Huangdi's Tomb *(Offline)*

ASSESS

Lesson Assessment: The Tomb of Qin Shi Huangdi (*Offline*)

You will complete an offline assessment covering the main objectives of this lesson. Your learning coach will score this assessment.

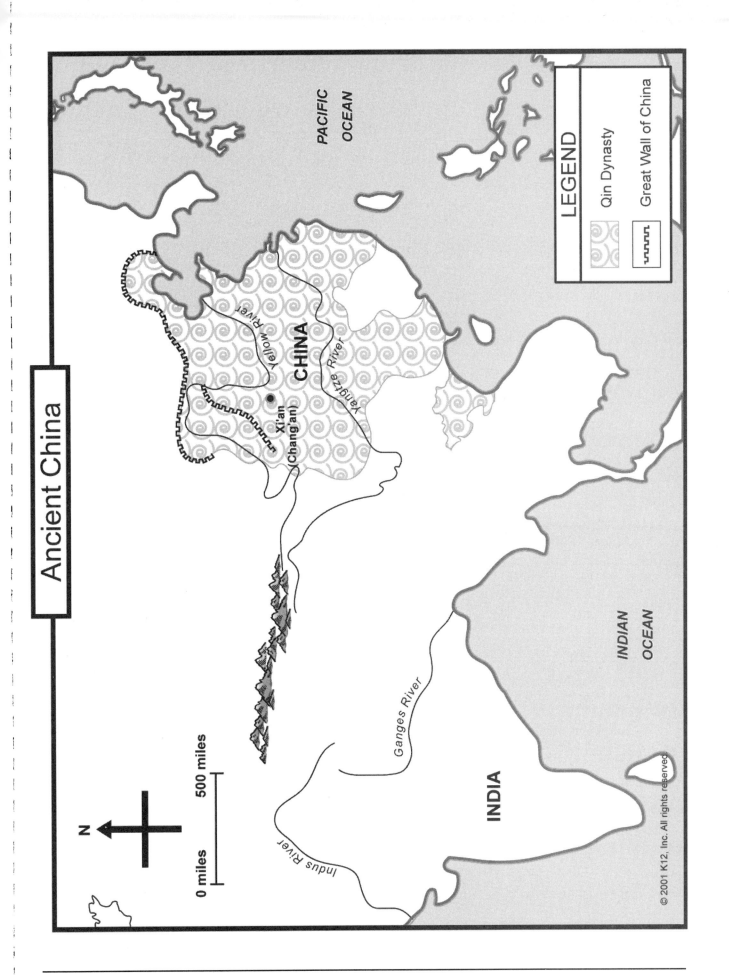

Ancient China

LEGEND

Qin Dynasty

Great Wall of China

PACIFIC OCEAN

CHINA

Yellow River

Yangtze River

Xi'an (Chang'an)

INDIA

Ganges River

Indus River

INDIAN OCEAN

N

500 miles

0 miles

Name _____ Date _____

Lesson Assessment

The Tomb of Qin Shi Huangdi

1. Besides the Great Wall, what else did Qin Shi Huangdi build?

2. What have archaeologists found in Qin Shi Huangdi's tomb?

Student Guide
Lesson 7: The Han Dynasty

Lesson Objectives

- Demonstrate mastery of important knowledge and skills in this unit.
- Explain that the Han Dynasty ushered in a time of peace and innovation.
- Identify the ancient Chinese as the civilization that invented paper.
- Locate the Yellow and Yangtze Rivers.
- Explain that the annual flooding of rivers allowed people to grow grain such as rice.
- Explain that the ancient Chinese discovered how to make silk.
- Define calligraphy as artistic handwriting.
- Identify Confucius as a teacher in ancient China.
- Explain that the Great Wall was built to keep invaders out of China.
- Describe Qin Shi Huangdi's underground tomb as being full of life-size clay soldiers and horses.

PREPARE

Approximate lesson time is 60 minutes.

Materials

For the Student

🖳 China Trades Her Goods activity sheet

crayons, 16 or more

pencils, no. 2

blender, electric

household items - dishpan, sponge

household items - stiff window screen

newspaper - or magazines

paper, 8 1/2" x 11"

tape, masking

water - hot

Keywords and Pronunciation

dynasty : A period of time (measured in hundreds of years) in which one family rules an empire.

LEARN
Activity 1: A Look Back *(Online)*

Activity 2: Han Dynasty *(Online)*

Activity 3. Optional: China Trades Her Goods *(Offline)*

Activity 4: Reviewing Unit Eight *(Online)*

ASSESS
Unit Assessment: Ancient China (*Offline*)
Complete an offline Unit Assessment. Your learning coach will score this part of the Assessment.

LEARN
Activity 5. Optional: Make Your Own Paper *(Offline)*

Name

Date

China Trades Her Goods

Unscramble the following words to show what China trades with her neighbors. Write the names of the places China traded with on the three blank lines.

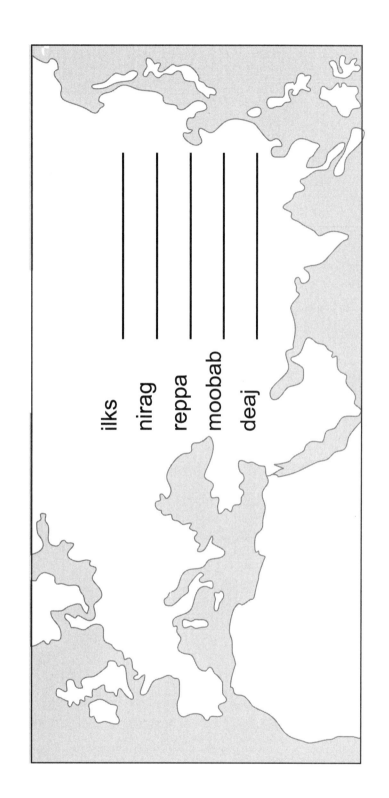

ilks

nirag

reppa

moobab

deaj

Name _____   Date _____

Ancient China

Select the one best answer. Shade or color the bubble for the answer you choose.

1. What allowed the ancient Chinese to grow grain such as rice?
    ○ hilly ground
    ○ yearly flooding of rivers
    ○ daily rains

2. What did the ancient Chinese discover how to make?
    ○ cotton
    ○ silk
    ○ yarn

3. The Chinese practiced *calligraphy*. Calligraphy is the art of
    ○ beautiful writing
    ○ graceful dancing
    ○ skillful weaving

4. What was Qin Shi Huangdi's underground tomb filled with?
    ○ mummies wrapped in cotton
    ○ hand-copied books
    ○ life-sized clay soldiers

5. Why was the Great Wall of China built?
    ○ to keep out water from the rivers
    ○ to keep Chinese farmers in
    ○ to keep invaders out

6. Which of these are the two main rivers in China?

○ Indus and Ganges

○ Yellow and Yangtze

○ Tigris and Euphrates

7. During the peaceful Han dynasty, what did the Chinese invent?

○ the plow

○ the chariot

○ paper

8. Who was Confucius?

○ a fierce warrior in ancient China

○ a wise teacher in ancient China

○ a cruel emperor in ancient China

Answer Keys

Lesson Assessment Answer Key

Life in Ancient Greece

Answers:

1. Greece is the area surrounding the Aegean Sea.
2. city-states
3. rocky and mountainous
4. no

Name _____   Date _____

Lesson Assessment Answer Key

The Greek Gods

Answers:

1. many
2. Mount Olympus
3. The Greek gods and goddesses were like people because they had to eat and sleep, they got angry or felt happy. They were unlike people because the lived forever and had amazing powers.
4. Zeus

Name _____   Date _____

Lesson Assessment

The Judgment of Paris

Answers:

1. Paris
2. The war started because of an argument over which goddess should receive the golden apple "for the fairest."
3. Aphrodite promised to give him the most beautiful woman in the world for his wife
4. Helen
5. to Troy
6. The Greeks fought the Trojans.

Lesson Assessment Answer Key

The Trojan War, Part 1

Answers:

1. Troy is in the Northwest corner of Asia Minor.
2. Priam

Lesson Assessment Answer Key

The Trojan War, Part 2

Answers:

1. They built a wooden horse and hid inside it.
2. The Greeks climbed out and set fire to the city of Troy.
3. Odysseus
4. the *Iliad*
5. the Greeks

Lesson Assessment Answer key

Homer's Great Greek Epics

Answers:

1. Homer
2. the Trojan War
3. Odysseus's long journey home

Lesson Assessment Answer Key

Let the Olympic Games Begin!

Answers:

1. ancient Greece
2. Athletic games such as running, wrestling, boxing, and chariot races.

Lesson Assessment Answer Key

Greek Myths: Arachne and King Midas

Answers:

1. myths
2. the golden touch--the power to turn whatever he touched into gold
3. spiders

Name _____   Date _____

Ancient Greece, Part I: The Land and Myths: Answer Key

Select the one best answer. Shade or color the bubble for the answer you choose.

1. This body of water was very important to the ancient Greeks. They sailed on its waters to travel and to trade with other lands.
   - ○ Nile River
   - ● Mediterranean Sea
   - ○ Euphrates River

2. What was Greece made up of?
   - ○ many good farms
   - ○ a single country
   - ● many city-states

3. What was the home of the Greek gods?
   - ● Mount Olympus
   - ○ Tower of Babel
   - ○ Crete

4. Who fought each other in the Trojan War?
   - ○ Greeks and Babylonians
   - ○ Trojans and Babylonians
   - ● Greeks and Trojans

5. What do we call stories that explain how things came to be?
   - ● myths
   - ○ poems
   - ○ fables

6. Which of these phrases comes from the Greek myth about King Midas?
   - ○ feather touch
   - ● golden touch
   - ○ golden eggs

7. What did the ancient Greeks believe in?
   - ○ one god
   - ● many gods
   - ○ three gods

8. What games did the ancient Greeks give the world?
   - ○ football
   - ○ soccer
   - ● Olympics

9. What were some Greek myths about?
   - ● heroes and monsters
   - ○ roads and temples
   - ○ land and water

10. Who was the king of the Greek gods?
    - ● Zeus
    - ○ Poseidon
    - ○ Homer

11. What does the poem called the *Iliad* tell the story of?
    - ● the Trojan War
    - ○ why we have seasons
    - ○ the adventures of Perseus

12. Who was the Greek poet of the *Odyssey*?
- ● Homer
- ○ Minos
- ○ Midas

13. What was the Trojan Horse?
- ○ a flying horse that lived on Mount Olympus
- ○ a giant magical horse tamed by the sea god, Poseidon
- ● a way for Greek soldiers to sneak inside and attack the city of Troy

14. Who was Perseus?
- ● a hero in a Greek myth
- ○ the author of a Greek myth
- ○ a monster in a Greek myth

Lesson Assessment Answer Key

Athena Gets a City

Answers:

1. Athena
2. an olive tree
3. wisdom
4. the sea

Lesson Assessment Answer Key

Athens and Democracy

Answers:

1. Athens is just below the second A in Attica.
2. the people rule
3. yes
4. they voted

Lesson Assessment Answer Key

Sparta: Be Brave and Strong

Answers:

1. Sparta is in Peloponnesus.
2. great warriors
3. toughness and bravery

Lesson Assessment Answer Key

Persia Rising: Darius on the Move

Answers:

1. The Persian Empires is the area denoted in the map key.
2. Darius
3. soldiers from Athens

Lesson Assessment Answer Key

The Battle of Marathon

Answers:

1. He decided to conquer Greece.
2. the Persians and the Greeks (or the Athenians)
3. the Greeks (or Athenians)
4. The Athenian's sent a messenger who ran from Marathon to Athens with the news of the Athenian victory.

Name _____ Date _____

Lesson Assessment Answer Key

The Battle of Thermopylae

Answers:

1. Persia and Greece
2. They stalled the Persians long enough for the Greeks to get their navy ready.
3. the Greeks

Name _____ Date _____

Lesson Assessment Answer Key

The Golden Age of Athens: Pericles

Answers:

1. Pericles
2. democracy
3.

   B.

4. the goddess Athena

Lesson Assessment Answer Key

Young Alexander

Answers:

1. Macedonia
2. Alexander's horse
3. They told Alexander that whoever could undo the Gordian Knot would have the world as his kingdom.
4. Alexander cut the Gordian Knot in half with his sword.
5. It showed that he had his mind made up to rule the world and he would not let anything stand in his way.

Name _____   Date _____

Ancient Greece, Part II: From Athens to Alexander
Answer Key

Select the one best answer. Shade or color the bubble for the answer you choose.

1. Who was the ancient Greek goddess of wisdom?
   - ○ Pericles
   - ● Athena
   - ○ Arachne

2. What does democracy mean?
   - ○ the kings rule
   - ● the people rule
   - ○ the soldiers rule

3. Who were Socrates, Plato, and Aristotle?
   - ● philosophers from Athens
   - ○ soldiers from Sparta
   - ○ senators from Rome

4. In which Greek city–state would you be more likely to find young boys training to become tough soldiers?
   - ○ Athens
   - ● Sparta

5. The Greeks fought a famous battle against the Persians, and then sent a runner to Athens to announce their victory. Today, athletes sometimes run a long race in memory of that battle and brave messenger. What was the name of the battle?
   - ○ Thermopylae
   - ● Marathon
   - ○ Olympus

6. What were the Spartans known for?
- ● toughness and bravery
- ○ wisdom and kindness
- ○ books and poems

7. How would you describe ancient Athens?
- ○ It was ruled by kings.
- ○ It was run by the Persians.
- ● It was a democracy.

8. Whom did the Greeks fight a war against and win?
- ○ the Macedonians
- ● the Persians
- ○ the Romans

9. What did Alexander the Great do?
- ● created a large empire by conquering many lands
- ○ ran a long distance with a message about the Battle of Marathon
- ○ fought against Darius at the Battle of Thermopylae

10. Look at these pictures. Draw a circle around the Parthenon.

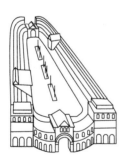  

Name _____ Date _____

Lesson Assessment Answer Key

The Mystery of Mohenjo-Daro

Answers:

1. The Indus River is labeled and on the north edge of India.

2. citadel cities

3. big, round mounds

Lesson Assessment Answer Key

Ancient Hinduism

Answers:

1. Hinduism

2. near the Indus River

3. many gods and goddesses

4. Brahman

Lesson Assessment Answer Key

The Ganges River

Answers:

1. The Indian subcontinent surrounds the country of India.

2. The Ganges River is on the northern side of the country of India.

3. Hinduism

Lesson Assessment Answer Key

The Ramayana

Answers:

1. a sacred book of the Hindus

2. Rama

3. an army of monkeys

Lesson Assessment Answer Key

Siddhartha Gautama: The Buddha

Answers:

1. a prince

2. the Buddha

3. Buddhism

4. Answers may very but should include details about how Siddhartha grew up protected from the outside world with great luxury. He was allowed to leave the palace and saw suffering. Siddhartha wandered the world for years until he became enlightened.

Name _____ Date _____

Lesson Assessment Answer Key

Asoka and the Spread of Buddhism

Answers:

1. Asoka

2. India

3. Asoka went to war and conquered other empires.

4. Buddhism

Name _____   Date _____

Ancient India: Answer Key

Select the one best answer. Shade or color the bubble for the answer you choose.

1. Which is the Indian religion that has many gods and goddesses?
   - ○ Vishnuism
   - ● Hinduism
   - ○ Judaism

2. What is the main reason that people settled down and built cities near the Indus River?
   - ○ because the river let them enjoy water sports
   - ● because the river provided water to drink and to grow crops
   - ○ because the river protected them against attackers

3. What are Brahma, Vishnu, and Shiva?
   - ● three main gods of Hinduism
   - ○ three rivers in India
   - ○ three cities in the Indus River valley

4. What river is sacred to Hindus?
   - ● Ganges
   - ○ Tigris
   - ○ Nile

5. Which of these is a sacred Hindu book?
   - ○ the Jataka
   - ● the Ramayana
   - ○ the Gautama

6. Who is known as the *Buddha* — the founder of Buddhism?
   - ○ Prince Rama
   - ○ Vishnu the Preserver
   - ● Siddartha Gautama

7. What did Asoka do?
   - ○ write the Jataka Tales
   - ● help spread Buddhism beyond India
   - ○ defeat an evil king

8. The map below shows two main rivers of ancient India. What are the names of these rivers?
   - ○ Tigris and Euphrates
   - ○ Nile and Niger
   - ● Indus and Ganges

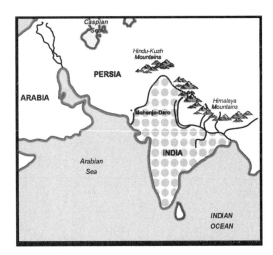

Lesson Assessment Answer Key

Farming in in Ancient China

Answers:

1. China is East of India
2. The Yellow River is above the word China on the map.
3. The Yangtze River is below the word China on the map.
4. The rivers gave water to plants. When they flooded, the rivers left behind rich soil.
5. rice

Lesson Assessment

Early China: The Discovery of Silk

Answers:

1. China
2. a silkworm cocoon
3. silk thread
4. They made lots of beautiful silk cloth.

Lesson Assessment Answer Key

Chinese Calligraphy

Answers:

1. They drew pictures called characters that stood for words.
2. Calligraphy is beautiful handwriting, or artistic handwriting.
3. A calligrapher is someone who writes with beautiful word-pictures.

Lesson Assessment Answer Key

Confucius: The Wise Teacher

Answers:

1. Confucius
2. They learned the sayings that he taught them.
3. how to live better lives

Name _____   Date _____

Lesson Assessment Answer Key

The Emperor Builds a Wall

Answers:

1. Qin Shi Huangdi
2. to keep his enemies out of China

Name _____   Date _____

Lesson Assessment Answer Key

The Tomb of Qin Shi Huangdi

Answers:

1. a huge underground tomb
2. clay soldiers with horses

Name _____   Date _____

Ancient China: Answer Key

Select the one best answer. Shade or color the bubble for the answer you choose.

1. What allowed the ancient Chinese to grow grain such as rice?
   - ○ hilly ground
   - ● yearly flooding of rivers
   - ○ daily rains

2. What did the ancient Chinese discover how to make?
   - ○ cotton
   - ● silk
   - ○ yarn

3. The Chinese practiced *calligraphy*. Calligraphy is the art of
   - ● beautiful writing
   - ○ graceful dancing
   - ○ skillful weaving

4. What was Qin Shi Huangdi's underground tomb filled with?
   - ○ mummies wrapped in cotton
   - ○ hand-copied books
   - ● life-sized clay soldiers

5. Why was the Great Wall of China built?
   - ○ to keep out water from the rivers
   - ○ to keep Chinese farmers in
   - ● to keep invaders out

6. Which of these are the two main rivers in China?
   - ○ Indus and Ganges
   - ● Yellow and Yangtze
   - ○ Tigris and Euphrates

7. During the peaceful Han dynasty, what did the Chinese invent?
   - ○ the plow
   - ○ the chariot
   - ● paper

8. Who was Confucius?
   - ○ a fierce warrior in ancient China
   - ● a wise teacher in ancient China
   - ○ a cruel emperor in ancient China